FIONA FARRELL is an award-winning novelist, playwright and poet. In 1995 she was the Katherine Mansfield Fellow in Menton and in 2006 she held the Rathcoola Residency in Ireland, where she wrote *The Pop-Up Book of Invasions* (Auckland University Press, 2007), shortlisted for the Montana New Zealand Book Awards. Fiona Farrell received the New Zealand Prime Minister's Award for Fiction in 2007. Her most recent novels are *Mr Allbones' Ferrets* (2007) and *Limestone* (2009), both nominated for the International IMPAC Dublin Literary Award. Farrell lives at Otanerito on Banks Peninsula, but spent 2011 in Dunedin as recipient of the Robert Burns Fellowship. She was in Christchurch on 4 September 2010 and at Dunsandel, driving south, on 22 February 2011.

The Broken Book

Fiona Farrell

AUCKLAND UNIVERSITY PRESS

First published 2011
Reprinted 2011 (twice), 2012 (twice)

Auckland University Press
University of Auckland
Private Bag 92019
Auckland 1142, New Zealand
www.press.auckland.ac.nz

© Fiona Farrell, 2011

ISBN 978 1 86940 576 2

Parts of this book were written while the author held the Robert Burns Fellowship at the
University of Otago; publication is kindly assisted by

ARTS COUNCIL OF NEW ZEALAND TOI AOTEAROA

National Library of New Zealand Cataloguing-in-Publication Data
Farrell, Fiona, 1947-
The broken book / Fiona Farrell.
ISBN 9781869405762
1. Farrell, Fiona, 1947- —Travel. 2. Earthquakes—Poetry. I. Title
NZ824.3—dc 22

Cover design: Athena Sommerfeld
Cover photographs: Trailsource.com, Inc. (front);
Soren Hald, Stone Collection, Getty Images (back).

Printed by Printlink Ltd, Wellington

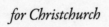

for Christchurch

The walks

The quake poems

Preamble

from *preambulare*: to walk before
May 2011

Last year I was writing a book. It was about walking: a travel book. My editor at Auckland University Press, Anna Hodge, had suggested it. My previous book had been a volume of poems, with copious notes, about time spent in Ireland. She thought travel suited me.

I decided I'd write about walking. It would be a simple book. What could be simpler than one foot in front of the other? I'd write about travelling on foot. It is, in my opinion, the very best mode of travel. So slow, so steady. The world slips into close focus: the few metres ahead, the next climb, the next corner, the row of ants marching across a sun-warmed step, the herd of caramel-coloured cows grazing in a buttercup field, heavy bells ringing.

Travelling by car is a swift swoop, suited to men with appointments elsewhere. It's fierce and competitive out there on the highway: people, perfectly pleasant no doubt when encountered on foot, become frantic. *I* become frantic. Stuck behind a campervan crawling up the hill into town, I can feel a ridiculous impatience: Come ON! Pass the truck! You've HEAPS of room and this is the only place you can get past for MILES! I am neither a good nor decent person driving a car. Some kind of fantasy takes over my head and hands: a person who rally-drives the Haute Corniche, wearing fingerless mittens for extra grip on the custom-made wheel. I have no idea where this person exists when I'm not in a car. I have never driven in a rally, nor wish to, and my notion of hell would be to stand on an embankment watching cars racing round bends and skidding into gravel. You can't even tell who is winning. So why is it, as I take the wheel of our Subaru to pop into town to pick up a bottle of milk and the paper, that this impatient neurotic competitive individual slips into my skin and fastens her helmet? Over unlikely greying hair? Who the hell is she? She is quite literally driven. Overwhelmed by the urge for speed, even if the object of that speed is a litre of trim, not the magnum of champagne gushing orgasmically over the losers.

When I travel on foot, I am calm. I am kind. I talk to strangers, enjoying their company. I am attentive to small children. I am not driven, but peaceably ambling to the rhythms of nature. I am rambling. My feet ramble. My mind rambles. The sun is on my face, the wind in my hair. The fantasy figure who slips into my skin then is romantic: someone in a high-waisted dress walking across heather-clad moorland with billowing clouds overhead. She's a pilgrim, a poet, someone from history or fairytale, setting out to seek her fortune.

She's also a relatively recent fantasy. For much of my life, walking was done from necessity. We walked when we were children because we didn't have a car until I was ten. We walked to school, which was just next door anyway, through a loose place in the corrugated-iron fence at the end of our section. A quick dash from the warm kitchen, clutching a piece of toast in one hand as the bell rang, through the fence, and I could be lined up with the others, all ready for Colonel Bogey and the march to class. (This has left me incapable of getting anywhere else on time. I still adhere to the belief that I can be eating toast and be wherever I am expected to be in the twinkling of an eye, like Superman. It's a dreadful legacy.) On Friday nights, my family walked downtown for the groceries and the library books, puffing back up the hill at nine o'clock with a pushchair loaded with supplies and kids demanding to be carried. At weekends, we didn't walk for recreation. Instead, my sister and I were taken out to visit my aunt and uncle on my dad's bike: a big heavy Raleigh with a seat on the carrier and another on the bar. Cycling was perfection: Dad puffing as he pedalled up Holmes Hill between high hedges of fluffy white hawthorn and the sensation of speed as we swooped back down in the evening, Dad cheerful after several hours of whisky and cribbage, the wind driving my hair back from my face on the way home to Sunday tea — proper shop-sliced white bread with raspberry jam and whipped cream.

Cycling was much to be preferred to walking. Walking was slog. A bore. A tedious tramp with my sixth-form geography class to view a glacier and hanging valleys and other dull geological features, goaded on by a young man whose muscled thighs strained at the khaki of his ranger's shorts. He looked like a boy scout. I loathed his silly legs, loathed the dripping bush, loathed the muddy track where my sneakers slipped and stuck. Loathed the glacier when we finally reached it, which was grubby and not, as I had hoped, pristine icy white. Loathed the clammy grip of my borrowed plastic parka. Loathed the way my legs ached that evening and for several days afterward.

What I wanted was a car, and when I was twenty-one and married we bought one. A grey Mini-Minor, in which we hurtled along English motorways, our friends pallid in the back seat as we raced past the spinning hubcaps of Eurolorries or attempted to change lanes round Marble Arch. I adored it, as I have loved all the cars I've owned since: the crimson Fiat with the kiddie seats in the back, the Ford station wagon that accommodated the family's bikes and tents, the beige 1967 Cortina of divorce, the trusty Subarus that now churn doggedly each winter through the snow on the hilltops of the Peninsula and bring us safely home to Otanerito in the valley.

It was not until I was middle aged that walking — walking as travel, walking for miles — really came into its own. When I was forty-eight, I went to live in Menton for six months. A fellowship took me to work for a year in the garden shed of the villa in which Katherine Mansfield had stayed for a few months and written 'Miss Brill' and 'The Daughters of the Late Colonel'. We lived in an apartment overlooking the town, up a steep little hill. We didn't have a car.

We walked instead. A network of tracks lined the hillside behind the town, the shadowy lines of the old footpaths that preceded the corniches, low, medium and, above them all, the multi-laned high road into Italy, flung across the ravine on towering trestles. The tracks marked old routes between tiny villages, overgrown olive groves, chapels with locked doors and leaves like flakes of dead skin piled deep on the porch. They wound between the stone walls of pastures carved from the steep limestone slopes and the rubble of former farm buildings. They zigzagged at a manageable slant, trodden into the ground by people who had had no choice but to walk and wanted to make as little necessary effort as possible. Sometimes there were flights of broad shallow steps, each stone tread worn to a smooth declivity at its centre by the passing of centuries of mule trains carrying salt from the coast to the interior. We followed in their hoofprints, up and down the hillsides, picking twigs of thyme and rosemary to flavour our casseroles. We walked between the little villages, finding the contour, approaching not with the roar of the sports car taking out each corner on the way up, but quietly, discreetly, past vegetable gardens where the tomatoes were strung on twine and the peas clung to crisscrossed bamboo stakes. When we became hot and sweaty, we dipped our hands in the laundry troughs set with such ingenuity to capture the flow of some mountain torrent rushing headlong to the Mediterranean far below. On its way, it had been briefly diverted to the task of cleaning sheets and bearing away the soapy sediment of living. There were sometimes towels and shirts strung on the wire fences, though the old communal customs were clearly giving way to whiteware and individual clothes driers.

As the weather that summer became warmer, we headed further inland, to the mountains of the Alpes-Maritimes. Our walks became longer: over hills to villages several hours' walk apart. We stayed in small hotels in near-deserted places where the empty streets echoed as we walked about after dinner and the cool mountain air smelled of damp stone and fallen rooms. It was as though the village was reverting to some earlier phase, of piled stone or before that: to the cave. Enough remained, though, to supply the necessities of life: a bakery, a school where children squealed as children everywhere squeal as they play. A church with mass once a month. New people were arriving. Sometimes in the hills we'd come upon their settlements: a caravan, a teepee with the usual confusion of dogs and children's toys, a pink plastic tractor lying on its side among the beans. At midsummer in Saorge, a quiet place ordinarily, the square suddenly filled with dreadlocks and people smoking dope and dancing all night to pipes and drums. The children ran wild along the balustrades above the sheer drop into a ravine where the Roya was a silver thread in the moonlight. They threw crackers at one another in the careless mayhem. In the morning, we stepped over bodies sleeping peaceably in the sunshine on the little round-backed bridge that led up to the scented pinewoods and the track to the next village.

I was enchanted. I had rediscovered walking. Walking at my own pace with no yapping ranger at my heels, it was not only possible to cover long distances — hundreds of kilometres, across the whole width of a country, across peninsulas and from one province to another — but to enjoy doing so. From then on, we spent nearly every penny we earned working over summer on going walking here or overseas.

I knew it was faintly ridiculous. Sometimes it involved a long initial flight across the whole width of the world: that trial by constriction in the economy section of Singapore Airlines. I'd look out at the vast red mass of Australia with its inscrutable squiggle of dry watercourses, at strange Singapore where millions roost in those white towers, at the sprinkled lights of the Indian subcontinent by night, while the cabin dozed behind eye masks and the little TV screens blinked with another rerun of *Friends*. Then it would be morning and we'd be passing high over all those wars and bombs and tensions, and then the land would crinkle and soften and disappear behind a web of grey cloud and there was Europe: London, or Paris, where we'd find the train. And the next day we'd start walking through a beech forest with bluebells or along one of those old French mule paths. Absurd. Self-indulgent. Pointless. Perfect.

So when Anna suggested a travel book, I thought, I'll write about walking. I'll think about places where I've walked. I'll write about the things I thought about when I was walking there. Because the way I think when I walk is different from the way I think when I am seated at my desk. The rhythm of my feet, the pendulum swing of my body, alters the way I think. My mind as well as my body wanders. My mind as well as my body rambles. I'll write down the things I saw on my walk, and the things I heard, the books I read on the way, the people we met, the food we ate. I'll remember it all and it will be like walking all over again.

I felt a little timid about writing like this: it would be non-fiction after all, and I've always written fiction. The demands of the story provide a useful cover. I don't like the feeling of being exposed, have never settled happily into the public side of being a writer. I like the quiet secluded side, concealed in a hut in a paddock in a valley a hundred kilometres from the nearest city. When I'm writing, I'm absorbed in solving a puzzle. I set up some difficulty — characters, a setting — and see if I can figure out how to make it all turn into fiction. The moment when that shifts into marketing — the launch, the interviews, the festival appearances, the panel discussions, the Hour With . . . — makes me jumpy with nerves. I cope by planning for weeks beforehand. I prepare. I over-prepare. I buy a new pair of shoes to look at when I'm tempted to run off the stage mid-session, and I get by. But it's not the part I like. It's not why I do this.

Writing non-fiction felt like another kind of exposure, a new kind of challenge. I was anxious, too, that this kind of travel account would seem banal. After all, there is nothing novel about walking. Thousands of people go walking. Our house is on a walking track. Over 40,000 people have stayed in our front room in the twenty years I've lived here. All summer I can hear their laughter down in the valley from my desk in the hut in the paddock. The magazines are filled with advertisements for walking trips in the Wairarapa with catered dinners, in England with a van to carry your bag, in Italy with optional trips to Assisi to see the frescoes or accommodation in a Tuscan villa. It's a favoured vacation choice of the middle-aged middle class. It's a passion fuelled by thousands of books: Aboriginal songlines and men walking away from the bank in their new sneakers have sold in their millions.

It's an expression of privilege. In countries where walking is the normal way to get about, it is not regarded as recreation.

This is why, I was told, walking tracks are few in Ireland: the era of people forced by poverty to walk the roads, carrying their spades on their shoulders, of children with bare feet blue with cold and studded with stone sores — all that is only a generation or two distant. Walking as recreation was more popular in wealthy England among people for whom country paths had some conveniently distant romantic allure. There's a whiff of muscular Christianity about it, the Bible class tramping group, the hairy-legged puritan insistence on mild discomfort and effort bringing its just reward.

I know all that, but still I love the simple sensation of moving steadily through a new landscape. It makes me feel grounded, steady, balanced on solid earth. My travel book would be about walking.

And then something happened that threw all that into disarray. I became anything but grounded. One night in September, the earth under my feet became anything but solid. I lost my balance.

This book has been written on either side of a couple of major earthquakes and more than 5000 aftershocks. That fact has left cracks across the surface of the text, rupturing it the way the earth ruptures. A muddy rift rips through the surface of pages that had been as orderly and purposeful as a flat Canterbury paddock with its stock rotations and regular rectangular borders of fencing wire.

Writing about walking is not so straightforward any more.

TWIGS

It's hard to walk on shaky
ground. Feet slip on
fractured stone, cracks
open where you least
expect. The signposts have
all been washed away, the
map's a blur, you've lost
the guide.

You must depend on small
signs: broken grass, a bird
that sings no no no, not
that way, try this way,
this way.

Sometimes you find twigs
laid out on a white page,
crisscross and up and
down. You pause and
puzzle. Then sidle off.

There is no option but
to head straight into
the sun, prodding as
old women do with
their irritable sticks,
feeling for solid spots.

A walk in the Cévennes

September 2009

You think to yourself: this is definitely the way to leave a town.

You walk down a narrow street before the place is quite awake. Cars are parked like birds at roost. Windows are shuttered. There is the sensation of people beginning to stir behind stone walls, of tumbled sheets, warm skin and the sweet slightly porcine reek of sleep. Your boots clump on cobbles. You share the street with skinny cats loping home with that furtive air that bespeaks nights spent in fornication and yowling dispute. They hug the walls, sidle through cat flaps to slip on their peaceable daytime selves, sleeping off excess on a sunny windowsill.

You pass under an archway, following broad shallow stairs downhill. There is the sound of water rushing through dodgy plumbing, the scent of soap and shampoo mingled with stale piss in concealed corners. There is the sound of birdsong and a bell chiming in the air above you. Beyond the walls of the sleeping houses there is a cathedral, big and dark, home to a small black Madonna who is carved from walnut wood and clad in glittering regalia. She bears a little black infant on her lap, sweetly impassive. Her feet protrude from beneath her jewelled gown in satin slippers in perfect first position. She wears a heavy crown. She sits in the dark cathedral hearing entreaties with her walnut ears, directing the faithful to the smooth slab of stone on the church floor where the sick may sleep and be cured of fever.

Behind the cathedral, on a skinny peak that looks like a raised admonitory finger, stands another Madonna. She is huge and red and was constructed in the nineteenth century from the remains of 213 cannons captured from the Russians at Sebastopol. She is red like chopped meat. She is red like dried blood. You can climb up through her massive body on an iron ladder. The metal walls are scribbled with graffiti. You can peer through little windows where Anne-Marie 2002 once stood to view the tiled roofs of the town rippling at the Virgin's feet like water around an intransigent boulder. The peak — a volcanic plug known locally and somewhat confusingly as a 'dyke', pronounced 'deek' — has had its tip chopped off to accommodate her bulk.

A kilometre or so to her right there is another dyke, more intact. At its tip perches a tiny chapel. It's perfect. It's unlikely — a child's drawing of a church on a mountain. It occupies its peak in accordance with the rule of imagination rather than more pragmatic engineering. A pale place with mermaids on the door lintel and faded murals and bleary lanthorn windows, masonry gripping with bare knuckles at worn stone. At its heart are three menhirs hinting at millennia of people puffing up the zigzag to the door long before Saint Michael came with his sword and bagged this peak, adding it to his inventory of pointy places: Monte Gargano in Italy, Mont-Saint-Michel in Brittany, Saint Michael's Mount in Cornwall. And this little chapel, Saint-Michel d'Aiguilhe: Saint Michael of the Needle.

It is one of the places pilgrims visit before setting off to view the remains of Saint James, fisherman and first of martyrs, which are interred in a silver coffin in a cathedral 1600 kilometres away. Not just a finger. Not just a hank of hair. Not just toenails — but the saint's entire body, mysteriously transported from Jerusalem in a boat without rudder or crew to the coast of Spain. Here, tradition has it, he remained buried for 800 years till an aged hermit named Pelago heard heavenly music and saw a star fall into the field where he lay. Campus Stellae. The field of the star. Compostella.

The star has drawn millions: half a million a year, at rough estimate, during the heyday of relics and pilgrimage between the eleventh and thirteenth centuries. There's a guide book written in the twelfth century by a monk, Aymeric Picaud of Poitiers, which outlines the route, mentions notable features and warns most particularly against the inhabitants of Navarre: 'full of malice, swarthy of complexion, ugly of appearance, depraved, perverse, despicable, disloyal, corrupt, lechers, drunkards and past masters of all forms of violence'. Frommer's couldn't have done better. He also lists the motives for pilgrimage. Some pilgrims walked for expiation, some with the instruments of their guilt — an axe, perhaps, used to commit murder — strapped to their bare bodies. Others walked to effect a cure. Or from religious devotion, or to gain absolution before death, or simply for a motive Picaud calls 'curiositas': to see what might be seen.

They are still coming in their thousands, following well-worn routes from Vézelay, Tours, Paris. Or from further afield: Brazil,

Quebec, New York. Their motives are basically unchanged, though perhaps differently expressed. Google 'Compostella' and the sites are filled with the blogs of satisfied Americans happy to have lost weight on pilgrimage and presumably anticipating a trouble-free afterlife.

And you could join them. You could leave this little town and walk south in the company of all the others you found gathered on the railway station yesterday at Saint-Étienne, waiting to take the branch line that leads to the walnut Madonna and the chapel on the needle. The group of Dutch women, ebullient in sturdy boots and backpacks. The small still group of Mexicans, the couple from Montreal in their matching lightweight hiking gear, the excitable man from Lyons who had worked for forty years as a tram driver and retired only last week and is now fulfilling an ambition first formed when he was serving as an altar boy in his local parish church. You could join them on the walk across the uplands to Moissac with its cloister of elegant stone prophets, all swan necks and long tendril fingers. You could climb the route over the Pyrenées into Spain, sleeping each night in dormitories with seventy other pilgrims snorting and rustling in their sleeping bags. You too could visit the church at Santo Domingo de la Calzada where the hen and rooster peck in their gilded cage above the nave, a reminder to the pilgrim of the medieval miracle in which a roasted hen rose from the platter, restored to life to expose a liar. You too could stand where millions have stood on the Mons Gaudii, the joyful mountain, for your first glimpse of the starry field. You too could stand in the cathedral of Saint James as the saint's relics emit whatever mysterious power it is such relics emit, while the

Botafumeiro, 120 pounds of solid silver, swings out across the nave, dispensing clouds of scented blessing.

But this morning, you are not choosing to walk out of town in the company of the Dutch women and the tram driver, though it is the stories of such pilgrims, not to mention little pigs and brave little tailors and knights and adventurers setting off to seek their fortunes, that make this feel so very much the right way to leave a town. Walking down narrow streets between stone walls, early one morning...

You are choosing another path entirely, one that leads to a different conclusion.

THE HORSE

Imagine a horse. A dapple
grey, standing in a field.
Eyes closed. Its lashes
demure, its pink nostrils
flaring on warm air. One
foot on point like a dancer
resting. The very image
of motion stilled. No jump
no dumdedum.

The horse dozes by a fence
and you, a small child,
sprawl on its back. Bare
legs straddle its warm
coat. Bare arms about the
neck of the beast. This beast
who lets you lie upon his back,
legs straddled in the sun.

And then there comes a
cloud, a cloud of flies no
bigger than a needle's
point, all prick and agitation.
They land upon the horse's
coat. His skin quivers. Not
all over. Just in that place
where the flies nick. Skin
quivers under bare legs.
He stamps one hoof.

Quiver and stamp.
Quiver and stamp on
a blue day and you small,
straddled across the back
of a big beast. And
that is how the earth is.

When I said we were going to go walking in the south of France, people presumed the walk to Compostella. 'You know . . .' they said. 'That one that whatshername — Shirley MacLaine — did.' I have friends who have indeed left Le Puy among the thousands heading south and west: one friend, who was once a Basilian monk, has walked — twice — from motives of faith and historical curiosity; another friend, whose marriage was in tatters, walked to clear her mind; a third joined a tour group to walk the most picturesque stretch in northern Spain, through the territory of Picaud's swarthy, unprincipled Navarrais, as an interesting vacation.

I did not want to follow them. I am simply not Catholic enough. I don't believe in sin. I don't believe in absolution, nor an afterlife, nor any of the tenets in which I was raised. But nor would I feel quite comfortable in joining millions who do, walking a route sanctioned by such long tradition and the fervour of faith. I didn't want to join the bloggers delighting in weight loss on the way to the Field of the Star.

So we chose a different path. We walked out one autumn morning from the little town, along a less-trodden route past the railway station and up a street lined with plain apartment blocks, following a guide book written not by a twelfth-century monk but by a scrawny querulous Scot. A less appealing book altogether, though it was in its time a bestseller: Robert Louis Stevenson's *Travels with a Donkey in the Cévennes*, an account of a journey on foot through the remote mountainous landscape of southern France.

In the autumn of 1878, disconsolate in love, Stevenson came to a village a few miles from Le Puy called Le Monastier where he purchased a donkey, Modestine: 'A diminutive she-ass, not much bigger than a dog, the colour of a mouse, with a kindly eye and a determined underjaw.' Modestine passed into the author's hands for 65 francs and a glass of brandy. He then loaded her with the necessities for a couple of weeks' walking: a sleeping sack, six feet square of green waterproof cart cloth lined with sheep's wool, especially sewn for him in Le Puy for the enormous sum of 80 francs. By day, Stevenson calculated the sack would act as a large pannier, containing a spirit lamp, a pan, a lantern, candles, two entire changes of warm clothing, books (including Peyrot's *Fathers of the Desert Vol. II* which has an ominously weighty ring to it), a railway rug, cakes of chocolate, tins of Bologna sausage, a leg of cold mutton, a bottle of Beaujolais, some bread (black and white) and an egg beater. When night fell, he would empty everything out and sleep in the sack beneath the stars.

Unsurprisingly, little Modestine struggled under the load. The sack, inexpertly packed, slid about and tumbled to the ground before they had gone more than a few yards. The poor beast was on heat, with blood under her tail. I don't know if being on heat feels like having a bad period, but I imagine it might be accompanied by the cramps and aches familiar to women. However, she shouldered the load and moved hesitantly off along the stony path leading away from Le Monastier. Pan and lantern and desert fathers balanced precariously on her narrow back, she picked her way downhill. She stumbled. She paused. She refused to move.

And then Stevenson began to beat her. For the next two weeks he drove her forward with switches he cut from hedgerows, and eventually with a piece of wood with a sharp protruding nail. And then he wrote about it.

'The poor brute's knees were trembling and her breathing was distressed,' he records. He beat her till his shoulders ached, though 'as a man worthy of the name of an Englishman it went against my conscience to lay my hand upon a female'. He beat her till 'blood appeared on Modestine's mouse-coloured wedge-like rump'. A passing muleteer — a professional drover and not, one supposes, given to undue sentimentality where animals were concerned — advised Stevenson to adjust the pack. 'It fatigues her,' he said. 'It fatigues her greatly.' But Stevenson carried on, until the donkey's legs were reduced to 'raw beef'. 'My heart', he writes, 'was as cold as a potato to my beast of burden.' The whimsical Dr Jekyll who so charmed the London literati and the Bohemians of Barbizon had turned nasty Mr Hyde.

It is astonishing that this record made a popular success of its perpetrator, but it did. *Travels with a Donkey* has sold millions. It is still in print, with illustrations and without, in several editions.

Stevenson seems to have been as startled as anyone at its reception. He had not set out to write a travel book when he left Paris for the south that summer. He had written an earlier account of a timid journey undertaken by canoe along the canals of northern France — *An Inland Voyage* — and that had found some popular readership. But the Cévennes attracted him more as the possible setting for an historical novel. The region had seen savage fighting in the seventeenth century between Catholic authority and dogged Protestants who, because they were poor and fought in their shirtsleeves, without uniforms, were called 'Camisards'. The conflict had had its due share of massacres and burnings and outrageous cruelty, as all such regional religious conflicts do. Stevenson had been raised in Edinburgh on similar tales of Scottish Covenanters. When he headed for those French hills, he hoped to find material suitable for some great sprawling romance in the manner of the writers he most admired: Scott, of course, and Hawthorne and Baudelaire — writers whom he sought as a self-confessed 'sedulous ape' to imitate. He came to the Cévennes to find setting and subject, to become a novelist.

His family had not intended this to be his profession. He had been expected instead to follow his father and grandfather into the manly business of constructing lighthouses, and, when that proved clearly hopeless, for a career in the law. But in childhood he had shown an impulse toward storytelling. He was a frail boy, taken to Menton on the Riviera for his lungs, a delicate little emperor who at six sat up in his convalescent bed dictating a history of Moses to his indulgent mother and nurse who dutifully wrote it all down.

As a young man, he adopted a writerly Bohemian air, scribbling at a table in Edinburgh bars where drinks were at hand and girls could be had for threepence. From there he moved across the Channel to that Mecca of all true Bohemians, Paris. There, supported by an allowance from his father, he hung about with the artists of Barbizon and Grez, all velvet jacket, floppy hair and flamboyant striped stockings. His biographer, Claire Harman, likens him at this phase to 'an intelligent hare'. At Barbizon he met and fell in love with an American woman ten years his senior, Fanny Osborne, who was hoping that a spell in France would turn her into an artist. When Fanny decided to return to California to perhaps reconcile with her husband, or perhaps set divorce proceedings in motion, Stevenson was distraught. Unlike his mother, his nurse and the countless men and women whom he had thus far charmed so effortlessly, Fanny might not, after all, choose him. The uncertainty drove him frantic. The only solution was action: to travel, as he writes in the preface to *Travels with a Donkey*, 'not to go anywhere, but to go … the great affair is to *move*'.

And move he does, driving Modestine along the stony track from Le Monastier to Le Bouchet-Saint-Nicolas, where he hopes to spend the night sleeping romantically in his sack beside a lake. But night falls and he blunders instead in the dark before chancing on a rustic inn. From Bouchet he lurches unsteadily south, losing his way frequently, spending an unwilling night in the open, ridiculed by peasants and little girls — 'impudent sly sluts', he calls them — before he arrives at the Trappist monastery of Notre-Dame-des-Neiges. For an Edinburgh Protestant, the very belly of the beast. To his surprise he is received with kindness and discovers something pleasantly 'manly' in the singing of the monks in chapel. He walks on through forests of chestnuts in tawny autumnal colour, and spends another night in the open where he regrets the absence of a companion 'who might lie near me in the starlight, silent and not moving, but ever within touch'. He spends a convivial evening at Chasserades in the company of men engaged to survey the line of a new railway, modernity making its way into these ancient hills.

At last he enters the true territory of the Camisard revolt, and things begin to look up. The Protestant inhabitants of the region have 'open telling faces' and 'a degree of intelligence' lacking in the Catholic population encountered earlier, and the women become better-looking by the day. He has, he writes, not seen a pretty one since Le Monastier, but in Pont de Montvert he shares a dining table with two passable ones — and as for the waitress! 'Clarisse waited the table with a heavy placable nonchalance, like a performing cow: her great grey eyes were steeped in amorous languor; her features, although fleshy, were of an original and accurate design; her mouth had a curl; her nostrils spoke of dainty pride . . . a face capable of strong emotion, and with training, it offered the promise of delicate sentiment.' A promise unrealised, for Clarisse disdains his attention.

And so our hero journeys on, along the valley of the Tarn toward Florac and over the peaks to Saint-Jean-du-Gard, noting handsome women and violent history, becoming more cheerful as he nears his destination and perhaps a letter *poste restante* from America. 'Perhaps someone was thinking of me in another country,' he writes wistfully. Perhaps 'love with folded wings' is contributing to his increasing sense of well-being. So, assessing women, arguing religion in bars, getting lost, scribbling in his journal, he walks south.

And beside him Modestine walks too. With her bloody tail and raw legs and painful load. There is a strange sexual edge to her mistreatment that suggests the source of Stevenson's fury. Quite early in the piece he records looking at her and seeing in her 'a faint resemblance to a lady of my acquaintance who formerly loaded me with kindness and this increased my horror at my cruelty'. Along the way, Modestine encounters a jack donkey by the roadside and their happy 'nickerings ... saddened me, as did everything that spoke of my donkey's sex'. Her femininity maddens him: her bleeding, her docility. He admits to horror, and to sadness, but never to restraint. The beatings continued relentlessly until the ostler at the inn in Saint-Jean-du-Gard declared Modestine unfit for travel.

Stevenson was bored anyway and eager for his letter at Alies, a few miles to the south. He put an end to his wandering, sold his 'ladyfriend' for half what he had paid for her only two weeks earlier, threw in a no doubt slightly grubby sleeping sack and all its contents, and took the coach. Once aboard, seated by the driver and rattling through a rocky valley, he permitted himself some regret. 'I became aware of my bereavement. I had lost Modestine. Up to that moment I had thought I hated her; but now she was gone. And oh, the difference to me!' Alone with the stage driver and some agreeable young male passengers, he wept a furtive tear. While Modestine, one hopes, went on to lead a less miserable donkey life.

This is the book that first established Stevenson as a popular writer, a reputation that increased with the publication of *Treasure Island*, *Dr Jekyll and Mr Hyde* and *Kidnapped*, until he had achieved the kind of international renown of a Lee Child, a Jeffrey Archer. He continued to travel, to *move*, seeking far and wide, like other writers plagued with ill health and weak chests — D. H. Lawrence, Mansfield — the perfect curative climate. Eventually he arrived in the Pacific in the devoted company of Fanny, her children, a couple of servants and his widowed mother who cheerfully chartered a luxury yacht in San Francisco for a seven-month ocean voyage. Stevenson's American publisher stumped up a massive £2000 advance (around $700,000 in modern currency) for another travel book, and off they went: island hopping from California to Samoa where they bought 400 acres on a hillside near Apia. There Stevenson established something part-colonial cacao plantation, part flimsy reworking of a Scottish baronial estate, complete with a house with the only fireplace in the tropics, and servants (he called them, of course, 'boys' — sometimes 'my black boys', 'obstructionist boys' when they were uncooperative or, more approvingly, 'amiable fawning dogs') whom he kitted out in kilts of Stevenson tartan. The 'boys' unpicked the kilts with their many heavy pleats to make more serviceable lavalava.

Comfortably ensconced at Vailima, he composed Scottish novels and minor pieces, commented on local politics and the jostling of America, Britain and Germany for regional domination, and wrote numerous letters to friends back in London in which he recorded, among other details, Fanny's increasingly wild 'hysterical fits'. These may have been syphilitic in origin. He died at forty-four, collapsing of a cerebral haemorrhage while helping Fanny make mayonnaise.

His fame soon declined. But eighty years after his death, the French Tourist Department was seeking ways to divert tourists into the *arrière-pays*, the backblocks of France. Stevenson's account of his walk through the Cévennes suggested a route: a 240-kilometre walking path from Le Puy to Saint-Jean-du-Gard, through the Velay, the Gevaudan and the Cévennes — a region that is most definitely *arrière*. Small stone villages cut off during the winter snows, empty houses smelling of damp stone, empty barns, a dry well-head at a crossroads, a locked church, tools smoothed by generations of use hanging in dusty little museums of regional life, the people long since moved off to the city and work. The route would stay off main roads, using old mule paths, the meandering web of droving roads, recent forestry tracks and a stretch of railway line that was in the process of energetic construction when Stevenson visited the region but was already decommissioned less than a hundred years later. The Chemin Stevenson would be a *Grande Randonnée*, one of the 37,000 kilometres of walking paths that crisscross France. There are guide books now in French and English, websites, maps and accommodation lists on the internet.

I had not read *Travels with a Donkey in the Cévennes* before we set out that autumn morning. In fact, I had never read anything at all by Stevenson, other than a classic comic version of *Treasure Island* when I was a child. It was boring. There were no girls. I simply liked the look of the hills on the websites, and the picture of a little village with a diminutive church and a humpback bridge over a mountain stream where a donkey bent her head to drink.

Modestine had become a marketing icon.

THE CRACK

Cracks open and stuff flies
up. Silt in dazzling fountains.
Grey stuff glitters in torch
light. The paddock has
become a garden of
illuminations. In San
Francisco, blue flame
danced from broken pipes.
In Kobe, rice fell from the
shelves like heavy rain.
In Haiti, disaster oozed
through holes in the
system. When the lights
went out, the rapes began.
The aid worker said you
could hear them. Cries
flew up from the dark
city, louder than any
bell ringing liberty,
equality and all that old
rubble.

And here, the refuges are
full. Women and children
on the run from the dazzle

of love, and the wreck of
ever after.

So — here you are, walking out of Le Puy one September
morning and it is perfect. The air is cool, the countryside made
up of humps and craters that are unmistakably volcanic, and
how odd that is! Volcanoes belong back home in shaky volatile
New Zealand, not here under fields of placid blonde cows.
You walk between stone-walled fields washed pale purple by
autumn crocuses or planted in a crop that looks like clover until
you look more closely and it's lentils! The lentils of Le Puy!
The best lentils with their *appellation controlée* on account of
their superior texture and capacity to hold their shape and not
turn to mush when cooked. And here they are, at home in their
native habitat rather than in those expensive little packets at the
deli. The sheep too are curiously different from the sheep you
know, those timid white creatures that inhabit the paddocks
round your home, their eyes glassy and fearful from repeated
shock. These sheep are small and lithe. Their wool is sooty black,
and their eyes are dark and fierce. They don't look like sheep that
would scatter at the sound of a farm bike.

That night you stay at a farmhouse. The farmer says the sheep
are reputed to be the descendants of animals brought here by
the Romans, but . . . He shrugs, pours his wine into his soup

and lifts his spoon. He is not a man for stories. The fact is that his sheep are strong enough to resist the winter cold and their meat is tender. You are eating it, stewed with courgettes and onions from a big practical garden with random bits of timber supporting dry vines and a pile of mulch for spreading. A real garden, not like the titivated plots of restored farmhouses in softer regions, their English country flowers in former pig troughs. There is a boy at the dinner table, a big simple man-boy with a moustache, who leans down to suck the soup from his bowl and laughs unexpectedly. A dog like a small ambulatory sofa lies under the table, his heavy tail thumping and brushing your bare legs. After dinner, you walk along the road in the moonlight to the corner where down in the valley there is a glimpse of the Loire which up here is a skinny little mountainy thing, gleaming. The dog pads behind, whimpering, anxious that you are leaving the safety of the fold after dark.

You walk to Le Bouchet-Saint-Nicolas where Stevenson lost his lake. The path crosses the red earth of a wide saucer-shaped caldera. That night, cows with their awkward bony hips jam the street outside the *bar tabac*. Herd after herd, driven by self-conscious girls in tight jeans and their mums in workaday pinafores, walk peaceably to their byres. The road out next morning smells of milk and shit and rich blue cheese, and your feet pick up the gait of cows: a steady simple pace that makes your pack squeak to a repeated rhythm that suggests random snatches of song. You find yourself humming as day follows day.

You sit in the sunshine at midday in stubbled fields, eating bread, cheese and apples, leaning against big rolls of prickly new-mown hay. As night falls, you zigzag down from the tops to some village where there is a *gite*, perhaps, in a former schoolhouse, now occupied by ebullient French hikers tucking into duck cracklings and beer. Or a hotel where the proprietor is nervous and forgetful and the cook is a flustered young woman who slams the pots and might possibly leave altogether before dishing up dessert, and there is that curious feeling of watching a drama with no idea of plot, context, subtle sub-text.

You come to Pradelles, where the soldier on the memorial in the sloping square wears an enamelled blue uniform and has brilliant red lips, pink cheeks and a deep golden tan. Not at all like the soldiers you know from the statues in the main streets at home who are cast in heroic serious bronze, with their lemon squeezer hats and their arms about their sons, their eyes fixed on the distant goal of sacrifice. You were always impressed by the distance they were about to travel as they said farewell: it was a frequent theme of the Anzac addresses. That these men had laid down their lives in a 'foreign field'. Their symbol was those flowers you wove into a wreath each year for the school gate. Always copper-coloured chrysanthemums from the garden, poked into a circle of cardboard cut from a Kornies packet. Pinned to the gate the flowers withered and died, as the young men had died, until the caretaker took all the wreaths and crosses and flung them into the school incinerator and that was Anzac over for another year.

Sometimes, when you are driving through some small settlement back home, you stop to look at the memorial. There it is, at the crossroads next to a ratty hotel, a couple of boarded-up shops with old sheets slung across their grimy windows. There's an empty school, the basketball court sprouting weeds. A church behind a shaggy macrocarpa hedge. You stop for a stretch, on your way to somewhere else. You walk about and read the names on the memorial, looking out for multiples: two, three, four of the same name. You imagine a family of boys embarking from this place, the farewell in the hall, the long pause, and then the telegrams. There are always so many names from the first war, fewer from the second, and then there are those ominous bare panels which look as if they are waiting for the next consignment.

But really, you think, looking at the little soldier in Pradelles in his blue uniform, would the war not have seemed almost as distant to him as to the young men from Kurow or Karamea? The flat and muddy northern fields, the mountains of Alsace must have seemed to him a foreign land. And his death would have been as dreadful, as absurd — bodies laid end to end in accord with army regulation, like country children top-and-tailing in a shared bed, the way we used to sleep when we stayed with our cousins at Waikouaiti. Only these dead soldiers were laid in rows of ten — ten on the bottom, ten above, and the twenty-first man laid crossways over the top. The wording on the memorials here is different too. At home, the words are noble: Sacrifice. The laying down of lives for Freedom. Age shall not weary them . . . Here, the language is plain. The memorials recall instead 'the children of this village'. Not heroes, but boys like the boys who are kicking a ball right now against a stone wall and riding their bikes hell for leather down the narrow alleyway past the Mairie.

You sit on the bed in your hotel in Pradelles, looking out over a valley of golden trees. The hotel is built into the town wall, on the very edge of a cliff. Birds whose names you don't know fly about the leafy tops beneath your window as the hills fade to blue. Their calls are strange. At home, at this time of day, the paradise ducks fly about, exchanging words in their different voices: the male going honk honk, the female sounding plaintive. Bellbirds echo one another up and down the valley, repeating the same little scrap of melody over and over, and there is the shriek of penguins coming in from a day's fishing. Here among the tweetings and whistlings the only sounds you recognise are a cuckoo, rocking back and forth in a creaky chair.

Days pass. You walk up forestry roads though pines, glad of the slab of shade but longing for the moment when you emerge onto the summit with its radio mast or ruin of a shepherd's bothy. You begin to recognise others who are also walking the Chemin Stevenson: they wave, stop and talk, call you over to share the duck cracklings and evening drink. The gentle economist from Paris, his skin so transparent the veins are a blue web, who walks for the good of his health. The young man who plans to turn his grandparents' farm in the Ardèche into an organic community and invite all his friends to live there and grow vegetables. The sturdy geriatric nurse from Tours, burned out by her job and desperate for some other career, but what? The lawyer who began walking after he had been buried in an avalanche in Switzerland: the week after his miraculous rescue he set out for Compostella, crossing France, crossing Spain, walking to Finisterre where Europe ran out and he was forced to turn around and walk back again, and he's still walking, east and north along those 37,000 kilometres of footpath, up to the Netherlands, down to the Mediterranean. Out in the breathable air, nervous at any restraint.

In Florac you walk into the square, following the sound of an oompah band, and find not uniforms and epaulettes but dreadlocked hippies in muslin pants who sweat and play the trumpet, the clarinet and an enormous wraparound sousaphone to a crowd of cheerful stoners and the tangled angels who are their children and their loping no-name dogs. The band plays well. You sit to listen, order coffee, the sun shines, the air is soft here in the lee of an immense limestone cliff. A spring surges from its foot, flowing under bridges to the river that runs down the valley. There is the sound of hooves approaching down the narrow street, and the jingle of bridle bells, and a row of mules driven by touselled young men and women wearing anklets trots rapidly past the bank, the menswear shop and the supermarket.

You walk through chestnut woods, the former staple of the region. Chestnut flour, chestnut bread, stewed chestnuts, baked chestnuts, chestnuts *glacés*, chestnut paste. The fruit lie thickly beneath the golden trees, each a small grenade in its prickly coat, and unharvested now that the smoky peasant cottage is a holiday home and the chestnut bread a tourist's delicacy. You startle a small black boar rootling luxuriously amid the remnants of a culture. He blunders off on stiff toy legs, reluctant to become paté. On stone walls, blue-green lizards flicker into crevices as you pass. That rustling could also be a viper, for they are common here. The guide book says if you are bitten, 'Do not panic'. Well, yes ... You nevertheless crash about more than is strictly necessary when stepping off the track to pee: bare bum, dry leaves, irritable snake 'dark green with characteristic zigzag stripes'. Do not panic.

You walk from Florac along the abandoned railway line, cut with such effort through tortuous country little more than a hundred years ago. The wooden ties are not yet rotten beneath your feet and there is the sense of time accelerating, time passing, technologies racing into oblivion, your own life becoming an artefact of no more than brief historical curiosity. You stay that night in a *gite* where the small elegant woman in the kitchen delivers cucumber salad, blanquette de veau and crème brûlée, and it's the best meal you've ever eaten. She's the owner's sister, taking care of the place while he attends a funeral. For thirteen years she was cook to Madame Pompidou. You lick your spoon like a president of France.

And at last you come to Saint-Jean-du-Gard, walking down from the Col de Saint-Pierre with its orientation tables at the highest point where the track crosses a road, pointing out all the other places you might walk to if you choose. The path downhill is slippery gravel and the trees have changed from chestnuts to olives. You are in the south suddenly. You join a busy road with buses and vans and motorbikes, the sound loud and peremptory after the squeak squeak of a pack, the puff of your own breath, the crunch of your own feet on stones. And so to a hotel where there are bedbugs that night, three busy brown bodies sucking your blood and off to their homes and their 200 babies in the bedhead. They squash between your fingernails with a satisfying crack and you sniff to see if they do indeed smell of coriander.

You'd read that somewhere. They don't. They smell like dirty socks.

And in the morning, like Stevenson, you take the coach, or, more accurately, you take a minibus. To the Roman temple and raked white gravel terraces of Nimes making eighteenth-century order from the mysteries of a spring. The water surges from below ground next to the temple, bubbles bursting on the surface in dark circles, and there is that sensation of hidden caverns and secretive passageways winding through limestone. Something going on unseen beneath your feet.

Then it's the TGV sweeping you back to the city, so fast it seems as if the entire country is standing still and holding its collective breath. And soon after that, the plane home: that extraordinary translocation that happens as you doze, from stone and autumn to weatherboard single storey and wide bare streets and trees in spring leaf and those bare buff hills toughing it out with the wind from the sea. And that clear light that makes all things plain, all things close, all things that speak of home.

And that's it.

A walk in France. Completely unremarkable. Thousands walk the Chemin Stevenson every year, for their health, or at a junction in their lives, or simply from that most valid of reasons, curiositas. It's not a pilgrimage, at least not one with a cathedral and a silver reliquary as its goal. But any walk can take on some of the functions of a pilgrimage. Any walk can have a revelation at its heart.

The Chemin Stevenson does not have a saint, but it does have a donkey.

A little donkey the colour of a mouse.

It's easy to forget the donkeys, to remember only the human companion. The man with the nailed stick, the Virgin carried toward Bethlehem, the man entering Jerusalem — though there was that poem we learned at school: *There was a shout about my ears / And palms before my feet.*

That was the poet's point exactly: it's so easy to overlook the donkey.

THE DOOR

Our door won't shut.
Anything might enter.
A man with a sack.
Water. Doubt. Or
the street light that
sways like a question
mark above the camellias.

Our door won't shut. It
won't keep the questions
out. It won't keep the
answers in. And all the
books might tumble
out, like bricks. Not
sentence, phrase or
meaning. Just bricks

with scratches.

I thought about Modestine while I was walking through autumn
in the Cévennes and reading Stevenson's bestseller for the first
time. I thought about autumn in New Zealand. How the wind
snatches yellow leaves from the willows by the creek and how they
spin and fall. Each year, we pick apples, storing them in cardboard
boxes to last till next summer. The spring on the hillside runs low,
trickling between lips of basalt. We gather walnuts and chestnuts
from trees planted in the nineteenth century by the Frenchman
who came to this valley and cut a farm from the bush. Normally
the trees crop heavily, but in a dry year each nut holds withered
kernels, wrinkled twins in a dusty womb.

It is the time of year when the young steers are taken from their
mothers. The farmer herds them into the yards to await the truck

that will carry them off for fattening and eventually for the kill. The steers mill about between high wooden fences, calling dolefully to their cow mothers who stand as close as they can, crowding into one corner of the paddock. They stretch their necks and call back, their cries echoing round the valley. The valley walls are basalt, the remains of two ancient lava flows. The stone reverberates with a kind of trumpeting chorale of lamentation.

The cows will stay there in the corner of the paddock, crammed against the fence, for days, long after the truck has rattled off up the road with its cargo. Once, the farmer tried to herd them back up onto the hillside as soon as the steers were in the yards. But the cows ran back, straight through fences, knocking over the posts and tearing their udders on barbed wire. It is better to leave them on the flat next to the yards to take their own time. They call all day and all night, stretching their soft grey necks to the empty air as the scent of their offspring slowly fades.

And eventually one of the older cows will move away up the hill, and one by one the others will follow. The bull, too, lumbering on his stumpy legs. They will wander back across the hillside where the grass is burned brown but will soon, with the winter rains, become palatable again. The spring will run clear. The cows' sides will fatten. They'll plump up with the unmistakable signs of pregnancy. And it will all begin again.

I thought about the cows as I walked through France in the company of a little donkey with raw legs. I thought about the forbearance of animals. How some permit us to take the milk intended for their own young and the wool intended to keep their own bodies warm, how they lend us their strength, how they permit us to harness their fundamental instincts, their fertility, the maternal affection with which they suckle and nurture their young. How they tolerate our cruelty, season after season.

We depend upon them, while despising their compliance. Animals that put up a decent fight receive our admiration: bears, wild boars, eagles. Lions become symbols of nations.

Cows have their admirers. There are those humpbacked cattle wreathed in marigolds, desultorily browsing the debris of Indian streets. There are those statues of Hathor, the Egyptian goddess of love, with her horned head and her big brown bovine eyes outlined in kohl. There are those exquisite cows grazing the limitless ancient grasslands of France sketched on limestone walls far underground. We walked to see them once, on another journey, climbing up a narrow road that wound across the face of a cliff. Niaux was a massive declivity with ticket booth and parking for a hundred cars. At its rear was a tiny door, the kind that exists in fairytales, through which the children march never to be seen again. It opened onto a dark landscape of little hills and mirror lakes through which we wound for a kilometre to where an ancient whirlpool had smoothed the rock to a pristine white apse. Now, that felt like a true pilgrimage: standing before the white wall with its icons, each animal in perfect outline down to the little tufts of fetlock hair. The whole bulk of the earth arches overhead, the animals' eyes glisten with tiny particles of quartz. And outside the cavern that night you look up and there is their trail, stretching across the width of the sky: the Milky Way that marks the path of the Indo-Europeans' great cow, wandering across the universe, her full udder spilling nourishing milk. Just as Polynesians imagined in the same ribbon of stars a spate of fat, sustaining tuna.

But right here, right now, cows are not objects of reverence. It's an insult: 'dumb cow'. And I am implicated too: I consume their milk, eat their meat with my sharp predatory canine teeth. Just as I eat the meat of the sheep whose desperation I have witnessed all my life: that agonised eye peering from the press of woolly bodies in the stock truck. Help me! it said to us without any doubt: to us seated with our ice-creams in our Austin Standard, impatient for the passing lane. Help me! to us holding our noses against the stink of fear and the trail of yellow piss staining hot summer tarmac.

As I became older and encountered other horrors, those trucks with their cram of desperate woolly bodies were part of it.

When we made our chrysanthemum wreaths each autumn and left them to hang and wither on the school gates, we watched jumpy old films of men marching up gangplanks onto troop ships off to that distant place they called The War. To mud and poppies and Anzac Cove and the going down of the sun. The men smiled and waved, but they looked exactly like sheep being loaded onto a truck. They probably bleated ironically too, the way New Zealanders sometimes do when in a single cheerful crowd being marshalled slowly forward: toward an entrance gate, an exit point.

When I was thirteen, I was reading one afternoon behind the

sofa, snug in the gap between upholstery and the bookshelves where my father's books were lined up: books about Ireland with strange round curly print, and books about boxing or the war with funny pictures of Johnny Anzac, and old leather-bound books from the secondhand shop in Dunedin with their strange pictures of animals in Africa and mighty waterfalls and fold-out maps that cracked along the folds and smelled of mice. It was quiet behind the sofa, safely distant from requests to pop round to the shop to pick up the bread or to set the table. I was reading a book. It was pleasant enough: about a little boy who lived in Germany and rode his black pony Hans about the hills, just as we rode our ponies around the hills of North Otago. And then I turned a page and it was no longer pleasant. The little boy became a soldier, commandant of a place called Auschwitz. There was a photograph of a pile of sticks. But when I looked more closely it wasn't sticks, but arms and legs. And there were other photos too, of people penned behind barbed wire and plain serviceable buildings and a high chimney, and those buildings would have been like the buildings out at Pukeuri which we passed whenever we drove to the river: plain serviceable buildings with the tall chimney that belched a stinking smoke that reeked of catfood and clung to hair and clothing whenever the wind blew over the town from the north. It was all muddled together and there was nothing to do but run from it, to jam it all back between the history of the 19th Battalion and *Kiwis with Gloves On* and run away into the clear open air of our back yard with its clothesline flapping clean shirts and pillowcases and the orderly green hillocks of potatoes. To breathe it all in — but the reek remained, persistent, unmistakable, beneath it all. It tainted everything.

Humans and animals could be treated with equal brutality, equal indifference. We ourselves were the children of a country colonised as one big farm. Our Pakeha ancestors had been dispatched here from overcrowded Europe by rulers who well understood that the way to keep a flock docile is to cull. They were men who owned land and had long experience in running an efficient estate. In the 1840s, when the stock in cramped cities and poverty-stricken rural hovels was becoming restless, catching the scent of European revolution, distant colonies offered a solution. Dispatch the young men to express their energy without causing domestic disruption in distant climes where they might return a profit in timber, wool or gold for the big London firms. Send after them young females, fit for breeding. Pen them in quarter-acre lots. And when unrest threatened once more at the start of the twentieth century, there was that more drastic cull of youth and vigour that brought the young man in his blue uniform in Pradelles together with the black-and-white men on the troopships to the same conclusion, laid ten by ten in foreign earth. My grandfather is there, killed by a sniper near Soissons in 1918. Just a name, listed missing. Raw flesh. Some scraps of bone.

And that was what I was thinking about as I walked through the autumn gold: about power and how it is taken and how it is conceded. I thought about donkeys and cows and how strange it is that creatures we once revered and drew in secret places gave power to us, a scrawny near-hairless primate. How odd it is that we get to determine where they walk in the world, and when they conceive their young and when they lose their young, and the time of their death.

Just once, one of the cows fought back. When the farmer came on his bike to round them up, she stood between him and his dogs and her own black-coated calf. She had the advantage of height, being uphill. She charged down through thistle and reeds and used her horns to flip the bike onto its side. The farmer scrambled clear just in time, though it was a close thing, he said. He dusted himself off while she lumbered back to her calf.

As I read Stevenson's bestseller, I wished that Modestine had had the cow's fury. I wished that she had kicked that irritable little Scottish writer and left him for dead with his books of old saints. I wished she had slipped her painful load and trotted off, leaving behind the leg of mutton and the egg beater and the wool-lined sleeping sack.

Off you run, Modestine. Off you run, girl, on your little knock-kneed legs, into the tawny autumn forest to forage with the wild pigs of the Cévennes. To find your jack, and mate, bear young, in the free high mountain air!

THE TARP

Our roof is broken.
Tiles cracked. The
chimney shattered.

The light gets in,
slivers of air slicing
to the soft pink heart.

Our roof is broken.
When the rain falls it
will scribble decay on
the ceiling. We will lie
in our white bed and
read above our heads
the end of things.

Our roof is broken.
We should cover it with
plastic, tie the tarp tight
at each corner so that
when the wind blows
it will not lift the lid
beneath which we lie
in our white bed, two
bare bald crinkled things.

We will look up as the roof
lifts. The air will come in,
tickling our stuff with
speculative fingers, rain
will fall on our bare faces.

But we are too timid for
the tarp. The ladder sways.

There is so far to fall.
We might never stop.

Then Hayden comes in
his new truck. He runs
up the rungs, walks on
broken tile. He ties the
tarp while we stand
below, looking up:
bare, bald, crinkled.

And that night we lie
in our white bed as
rain falls

pip

pip

pip

on Hayden's new tarpaulin.

A walk to the Winter Palace

Menton, September 2009

A warm day in late September. September is perfect in either hemisphere. In the southern hemisphere it is skippy lambs and apple blossom interleaved with sodden snow and flood and those little woolly bodies, still tinted yolk yellow, stiff legged in muddy paddocks. And gulls fly in, skidding down the wind, shaven heads and beaks like flick knives, for a decent feed.

September in the north, in Menton, is the fag end of summer, the air occasionally riven by astonishing thunderstorms, or utterly motionless in that strange foreign fashion. At home, the air is never so still. There is always some tickling at willow leaves, always a jittery breath on bare skin, that restlessness of gaunt sea-blown latitudes. But here, where the Riviera comes to an abrupt end against the solid wall of the Alpes-Maritimes, the air sags over mouth and nose like a heavy woollen blanket. The hills rise above the town in steep crags of white limestone stained red with ochre. At sunset they turn pink: an old-fashioned colour. Ashes of roses. The exact tint of blood stains on white linen once that linen has been washed many times and hung to bleach in brilliant light.

The limestone radiates a perceptible steady warmth. A bony reef composed not from some inanimate substance — volcanic crystals, sand — but from the remains of countless tiny living things with whom we share a common ancestry, 300 million or so great-grandparents ago. Billions of sea creatures like the bryozoa, each of which lived within its own little box with a hinged lid that could be flipped up for feeding. They are still with us, doing exactly that on the margins of the world's oceans, flipping up their lids, drawing food particles into their mouths with fine wafting cilia. Each a tiny being with gut and bum and a simple nervous system — not so very different, really, from ourselves. Creatures that live for a few weeks before performing their clever trick.

They appear to die.

Within their little box they rot to brown sludge. For a spell they remain inert. Then, miraculously, they stir to life once more. They begin to take on their former shape: gut, bum, nerves. The creature is reborn. Three times they do this, a process called 'cyclical degeneration and regeneration', before they die for good. The shelly box dissolves. Some particles go to form a new box for the young who have budded from their parent's body. The remainder filter down through the tidal waters to settle and form a reef like the one that has risen from beneath a primeval sea and now towers above Menton. The town is overlooked by the remains of creatures who acquired the knack of resurrection.

The reef is sharply sculpted into peaks and bluffs and caverns which offered shelter to some of our more recent ancestors. Their artefacts are on display in the museum at the top of avenue Lorédan Larchey: gnawed bones, chipped flints, the nubs of red ochre with which they ornamented their dead, the charred remains of a hearth reputed to be the earliest in Europe. The cabinets are dimly lit dioramas with life-size figures of early humans chipping stone and scraping animal skins. There is a plaster replica of the one known as Menton Man as he was laid out for burial 30,000 years ago in the Grotte de Cavillon wearing a headdress of threaded shells and reindeer teeth.

Thousands of years, thousands of lives lived on the limestone hillsides above this coast which is now as densely crowded as some tidal reef with the mansions of Cap-Martin and Roquebrune, the apartment blocks of Garavan, the casino and toytown castle of Monaco. In one cave only a few hundred metres from the casino and the castle were found the bones of an old woman, tenderly furled about the bones of a small child. In another — Terra Amata — hunters had strewn a litter of chewed bone. They had feasted on deer, rabbits and the occasional rhinoceros before pooing about their shelter with a cheerful, dog-like lack of restraint. From pollen particles in their fossilised turds — 'coprolites' to the more fastidious — archaeologists surmise a summer encampment 400,000 years ago when the broom was in flower and all the resinous woody plants of the garigue that still scent the rocky slopes.

In one museum cabinet there is a line-up of thumb-sized goddesses carved from bone and stone, plump with unfashionable rounded bums and heavy breasts, and the hint of some unknowable faith. Another cabinet reproduces designs scratched onto the rocks on the summit of Mont Bego, a few kilometres inland. Back in 1995, when I had the Mansfield Fellowship and lived in Menton, we walked up to view the originals, a steady plod through pine forest and out after a couple of hours onto the bare open tops. The air was cool and lively after the stifling heat of the coast. Clouds banked up above the ridges, and absurd little marmots squeaked in warning then uptailed and popped below ground. The rocks here were polished to a high silky finish by ice. They formed the kind of smooth even slabs irresistible to humans who must scratch and leave their mark, and some time in the distant past — the Tourist Department guessed Bronze Age — people had done just that. Everywhere, the rock surfaces were covered in tiny images. Cows' horns, dancing figures with arms upraised, arrow heads, spirals, rows of tally marks, rectangles carefully subdivided, dotted lines, and the head and shoulders of a bearded man holding aloft two jagged thunderbolts. We walked between the rock slabs as if down an avenue, to twin tarns of still dark water. Thunder rumbled round the tops, like iron wheels circling, and lightning danced along the ridges, driving us down like errant children to the safety of the pine trees.

Menton is such an old place. Humans have lived here, eating rhino and threading shells, giving birth, believing whatever it was they believed, walking about these hills on their big bare feet, calloused and stone bruised, the soles covered in toughened skin. Like our feet when we were children and ran about all summer without shoes. 'Summer feet' we called them, back in North Otago, when they'd become hard like a pony's hooves or a pig's trotters, impervious to thistle prick and river shingle. 'We've got our summer feet!' It felt like a kind of achievement.

There came a mighty sound
and on the seventh floor
the sleepers woke. The man
who has hung his daily skin
on the rack, the woman whose
mouth is a pink hole, the tour
group who are looking for
the light, the lovers who lie
tangled in 500 white threads.

They rise at the clap of dinner
trays and chocolates, tooth
mugs and shower caps, as all
the doors fall open on the
seventh floor. The sleepers
come forth blinking. They
emerge, bare crinkled things
from the crevices of the
seventh floor. Naked on the
carpet of little stars that light
the way to the stairs,
the empty shaft
that just goes
down
and
down.

So here we are on this autumn day, two more little humans in the long procession who have walked up the lower slopes of the Alpes-Maritimes. The bluffs loom overhead, walling off the ends of streets and the gaps between buildings. We are walking toward them, away from the beaches where the tourists still sunbathe though the shops are already displaying woollen jackets and winter boots. The sunbathers sprawl in the last of the summer's sun, on shingle and sand that has been trucked in by the council to cover the harsh reality of sharp coastal rocks. They doze on their manufactured beach, buffed and brown like so many leather handbags laid out for inspection. The sand is white and soft as blown ash. The high-tide line is made up of tiny shells and thousands of cigarette butts. When we lived here and swam every morning, there was a panty liner that floated in the lee of the breakwater. We began to look for it, the way you begin to look out for the elastoplast on the bottom of the swimming pool as you do lengths. It floated there, white and undefiled, all summer: a triumph of plastic technology. I wrote a poem that began

> *Nothing could be finer*
> *Than to be a panty liner*
> *On the Côte d'Azur . . .*

The sunbathers lie on the white beach while, at their feet, the mountains continue their vertiginous descent. Down, down, down beneath the swimmers thrashing out to the raft and back. Down into the dark submarine landscape that exists off this shore as a shadowy negative to the sunny place depicted on the postcards along the rue Saint-Michel. Up here, in the world of light, the crags are home to sweet villages with tubs of pink pelargoniums. Menton itself perches, perky, at the point where France stops and other customs, other words, begin. It occupies the very tip of the country like so many teacups arranged on a narrow shelf about the pepperpot tower of Saint Michael's church.

Today is the saint's feast day. The bells began ringing early. The church was packed for solemn mass, the air heavy with incense and doleful hymns. Now the parishioners are at lunch down on the waterfront. There's a band, and plump dignitaries in suits. There are pancakes of the region and a man announcing things, as there always is at such events, over an impenetrable loudspeaker system.

We walk to the sound of municipal festivity down Lorédan Larchey, where a stream has been channelled to form a narrow fountain running the length of the street. People sit beside it in the evenings to talk, and a gang of boys gathers to share a single scooter on which they take turns to rip around the streets, rearing on one wheel to impress. The village rises steeply from the shore in alleys of tall houses following wilful contours, up steps, under arches, opening onto a square with patterned stones. We turn onto rue Saint-Michel with its clutter of restaurants selling *salades composées* and fixed-price lunches to the tourists. Past the shops selling tablecloths and aprons and teatowels in Provençal blue and yellow, patterned with olive leaves and lemons. Past the ice-cream carts with their tubs of chocolate and vivid pistachio. Past the shop with its window display of candied fruits, sticky and achingly sweet. The streets are filled with tourists in snowy white resort wear and flinty little women with apricot-tinted terriers on an indulgent leash.

The street is a shady canyon between stone buildings, but as we turn into the avenue de Sospel, the sun slams down like a pot lid. The parochial loudspeaker and the band melt into the everyday whine of scooters racing away from the lights, the heehaw of an ambulance, the rattle of the 1.05 from Ventimiglia crossing the railway bridge and slowing for the station. We walk up the wide avenue past the library where there is a special display marking the anniversary of the Mansfield Fellowship. For forty years, New Zealand writers have been coming here to live and work for a few months in the town where Mansfield wrote 'The Daughters of the Late Colonel'. The library windows have the familiar photos of Mansfield at her desk, Mansfield seated on the deckchair on the terrace of the Villa Isola Bella in Garavan, looking like a wild kitten, trapped. There is a list of Mansfield Fellows, including Bille Monhire, Wity Ihimaera and Migel Cox — and a rust-coloured shawl that once belonged to Mansfield displayed in a glass cabinet like a saint's handkerchief. That is why I am here in Menton on this September day: for the anniversary round of mayoral receptions, dinners, poetry readings, and a conference: 'Celebrating Katherine Mansfield: A Symposium Organised by the Katherine Mansfield Society'. Five days of talks dedicated to the writer's memory. Fifty Mansfield scholars gathered in the Villa Serena overlooking the Mediterranean.

I once spent two years of my life poring over another writer's work: my subject was T. S. Eliot. *Sweeney Agonistes*. The play he began, then put aside when he became High Anglican and pompous. I remember enjoying the process. Examining the pencil draft of the play in the odd intimacy of the great man's own handwriting, the faintly absurd pleasure at discovering that he had intended a very different structure from the one normally published. (He had written out of sequence, in bits, but in print *Sweeney Agonistes* appears run on, giving a fictive coherence to the text.) I spent two years on a thesis and planned to write an article. But one day in the Cambridge University Library I suddenly felt breathless. There was a list of articles about Eliot, a huge list of rocks piled one by one on the monument. He was a cruel man, a vain man, one of those men whose life was too comfy, coddled by women and fame, too easy once he'd taken on that preachy complacent faith.

There was the smell of freshly baked scones in the library, from the café downstairs. The smell was rich and buttery. Eliot on the other hand gave off a whiff of old shoes, tweed suits in closed cupboards, a plump poet farting surreptitiously after a good collegial lunch — he'd have called it 'luncheon' with that precision of the Midwestern boy taking on English ways. I shut the book, laid Eliot aside for ever, and went and had a scone. Then I rode my bike back to the terrace house we had rented for the year, stopping only to put an ad in the YMCA for a composer. I'd find a collaborator. I had an idea for a musical for children. We'd work on it together. And bugger Eliot. And just to prove that this was definitely the correct way to go about things, there was Donna, Harvard music graduate, fresh from a summer working with Joe Papp in New York, temping at the Y and desperate to escape filing. It felt wonderful.

In Menton in 2009 I sat on the bed in the hotel on avenue Lorédan Larchey, just across the road from the museum, scanning the conference proposals. 'From Flagrant to Fragrant: (Re)Inventing Katherine Mansfield. This paper will chart the mythologizing process and provide evidence for the serious misinterpretation of this iconic literary figure in France.' Or 'This paper examines the ways representations of space and place work in Mansfield's fiction to articulate an aesthetic of risk.' The members of the Mansfield Society seemed to be excited and disputatious academics. Some of the women had had their hair clipped in blunt Mansfieldian bobs. They sat over their *salades composées* in the evenings on the rue Saint-Michel, playing facts like conkers. Whoever had the most resistant fact won hands down. It was hot. The air hung heavy over my mouth. It was like being stuck in a car on a very long journey with closed windows and lots of people talking. I should have attended the conference. But I went for a walk instead.

We walked to the Winter Palace.

THE FALL OF EMPIRES

This is how empires fall.
Book by book, word by word.
The shelves slewed sideways

blocking access. The library
is wrecked. The theatre is
invaded by cats. The little
golden goats are trapped
in their silver thickets and
the lions who crouched
when princes passed.

Empires fall on sunny
days, leaving columns
like broken teeth, grinning
in a desert. The road to the
marketplace is buried by
ash.

Empires are choked
by flowers while little
people creep in the leaf
litter. Everyone forgets
the words for things: like
cup, and progress. The
lockers in the school
hall gape.

Empires fall to sleep on
the point of a needle. They
slump.

We had seen the Winter Palace often enough from a distance. It occupies a spur just across the hillside from the Palais Lutetia where we lived in 1995. A massive rectangular slab of white ornamented with decorative golden scallops like some festive cake. The Palais Lutetia was painted pelargonium pink, its only nod to fantasy a vaguely Egyptian turret on one corner. It was small and plain compared to the Winter Palace. Behind its snowy bulk we could just make out the corner of the even more massive Riviera Palace, the original of the big hotels that sprang up all over the hillsides of Menton overnight, like fungi in a fertile field, to house the sick of Europe's beautiful epoch.

The Riviera came first, a pseudo-Baroque concoction of which its builder was so proud that he had his name engraved with an Art Nouveau flourish across the façade: J A WIDMER 1898–1910. Its walls were palest ochre and eggshell blue, with extravagant plaster swags by the curiously named (to a New Zealand ear at any rate) Guillaume Cerutti-Maori, the motifs depicting all the nations of Europe. Inside, the décor was as ornate, with frescoes of putti and wild animals and a sweeping *La Traviata* of a staircase. Outside, the gardens were filled with the palm trees which now seem quite at home on the Côte d'Azur, and unremarkable, but which were once enormously exotic, a fitting setting for the theatricality of the hotels. The Riviera and the Winter Palace had dozens of luxurious rooms. They had central heating and electrical elevators. They were constructed moreover on the most desirable location in Menton, only metres away from that most wonderful convenience, an international railway line. More modest establishments were relegated to the seafront with its uncomfortable breezes: the Balmoral, the

Windsor, the Orient Palace with its Moorish windows and its twin gatekeepers' lodges, each sporting a golden Ali Baba cupola. Sixty hotels, constructed to impress and house the tubercular tourists of England, Russia, Holland, Germany, during the brief period when Menton and those other impoverished and insignificant fishing villages, Nice and Cannes, were transformed into one vast coastal sanatorium.

Sanatorium ...

The word has a cloying sound. Some sticky residue of vulnerable human flesh, some whiff of mortal decay like the green stains on a bath at an elegant spa. Beyond the white linen and the dining room's string quartet, beyond the botanical gardens and the casino, beneath the scent of *eau des violettes*, there lurks the stink of sulphur that is also the signature of rot and putrefaction.

Sanatorium ...

It conjures up rows of pale children lying on deckchairs to receive their measure of health-giving sunlight. It conjures up Mimì knocking at the door with her tiny frozen hand. And Hans Castorp beneath his cosy woollen blanket among the pine trees on the magic mountain. It conjures up the laughter of frail youth, dancing.

Sanatorium ...

It's a word from childhood. When my mother was twenty-one she went to a sanatorium. She went 'up to Waipiata' to nurse her younger brother, Rob, who had TB. He was her favourite. Dark haired, 'reckless', she said, and musical. He played the violin 'by ear', which was much to be preferred to the way we played, plodding after the notes in a book with icy fingers on the piano in our front room, the china cabinet tinkling in uneven accompaniment. Rob could play the tunes from the pictures after hearing them only once.

He was clever, too, the first in the family to go to university. He was going to be a lawyer. But in his first year he shared a room with another young man, also musical, also planning to be a lawyer. They rode down Cumberland Street on Rob's motorbike, and played duets at the Savoy on Saturday evenings to make some extra money, Rob on violin, the other young man on piano. All that first winter the young man coughed. And somehow the disease took flight. It flew across that chilly shared room and found the weak place in Rob's spine, the place where he had been injured when he hit a fallen tree one night riding his motorbike down the Kilmog in a storm. Something had pierced his back, leaving a weak place, a portal through which disease might enter. We knew the bike. It was out in the barn at my aunt's place. It had curling handlebars and a little Indian head on the front, festooned with cobwebs. On wet days we sat on its cracked saddle, clutching the handlebars and pretending to ride. Among the hay bales and skinny feral cats we rode to distant places. We rode recklessly, full tilt through wind and storm, we were impervious to harm . . .

The disease flew like a swift little bird and nested in Rob's spine. There, it began to grow. (We imagined a kind of rot, like the damp rot in the weatherboards behind the washhouse, white paint barely concealing disorder and decay, and smelling of mushrooms.) The TB grew and Rob's spine rotted, and our mother took leave from her job at Oamaru Public and went 'up to Waipiata' to nurse him. She seemed to be immune to the disease herself, an immunity I had somehow inherited. (I was one of the few children at Oamaru South School who did not have to join the orderly row for the health nurse when she came with her scary needle.) Our mother had nursed people with TB and not succumbed as others did, dying as nurses were called upon to do: heroes to their vocation in their uniforms, medals and stiff white veils. But our mother remained well, and when Rob became ill, she nursed him. We knew what that would have meant: a stout campaign, with fresh air, good food, a rigorous and regular routine. And, in time, he did indeed seem to recover. He returned home, to the farm at Merton, to convalesce. But within a few weeks it became clear that the disease had not been defeated after all. A devious enemy, it had merely regrouped. It had taken up a new redoubt in Rob's brain, and there it lodged and made him mad. It destroyed whatever part of a man it is that enables him to play the violin by ear and reproduce all the tunes from the pictures. It destroyed speech and reason, and turned him into the shambling figure in his doleful brown cardigan who shuffled out to the car from a villa at Cherry Farm for Sunday church and lunch.

Rob had 'gone mental' like the other alarming men who shouted unexpectedly or sat staring at the pallid linoleum as if it might suddenly break into flowers. When Rob climbed into the car, he smelled of stewed cabbage and pee. We turned side on to look out the windows, and tried not to breathe too deeply.

Sanatorium . . .

Somewhere in the word is a woman hugging her shambling brother and the seesaw squawk of a violin playing something that might be 'Jingle Bells' or 'Happy Birthday', because she has said to him after roast lamb and jelly and cream, 'Go on, Rob. Give us a tune.' She has handed him the violin. He remembers how to hold it, and how to draw the bow across the strings. The sound could be 'Three Blind Mice'.

Sanatorium . . .

A queasy word, with a peculiar resemblance to 'Sanitarium' on the peanut butter jar and the Weet-Bix packet. The word lent a faintly dubious taint to substances intended to make us strong and 'build up our resistance'. We did a lot of things to build up our resistance: swimming in the sea when it was only just warm enough, sleeping winter and summer with the window open, swallowing a daily spoonful of malt extract and little leathery capsules of halibut oil. Our bodies were small bastions under constant siege. We must be vigilant. We must never 'overdo things' nor permit ourselves to get 'run down'. We must never study too rigorously, for we like Rob could 'crack up'. Our brains we imagined as frail things, delicate as bone china. They could so easily become weighted down with too much fact and crack under the strain.

Sanatorium . . .

The winter before we came to Menton and set out to walk to

the Winter Palace, I had visited Waipiata for the first time. A hoar frost lay thick over the land, obscuring names we knew were there from the map. The Rough Ridge, the peaks of the Raggedy Range stood about us, just out of sight. Frost draped the willow trees in filigree of brilliant white. It created Baroque swags from sagging fences and telegraph wires. Cows huddled black and white and disconsolate beneath small clouds of their own breathing. All sound was muffled, all colour leached from roadside grass. We had no sense of north or south. We were simply following a narrow strip of damp black tarmac. From time to time, cars emerged from the fog in a blur of headlights and swished past into silence. Then we turned a corner and the road rose a little, and suddenly we burst into sunlight like swimmers breaking up through heavy surf. There was a sign by the roadside: Waipiata. A name from childhood. Let's go there.

The road wound along a hillside, the valley below invisible in its thick meringue whip of white fog. Up here the light was clean, and the air cold and crisp as water from a spring. There were some buildings to our left, big low-slung wooden buildings with that pre-war Ministry of Works solidity, gum trees, an open gateway.

The complex is no longer a sanatorium. That ended back in 1961 when such places were closing all over the world. During the war, a poorly paid research student in the Department of Soil Microbiology at Rutgers University had discovered a cure for tuberculosis in a chicken's throat, and the world changed. Waipiata's wooden wards and bungalows were no longer needed to house the sick. Their broad verandahs emptied of beds and reclining chairs — the Adirondack chairs specially designed for tubercular patients confined to months of total rest and fresh air. The bustle in the laundry, the dining room, the kitchen with its massive ovens for the preparation of restorative meals heavy on cream and butter and all things necessary to build up the resistance of bodies fallen to siege — all this had disappeared as if into heavy fog. A white dream. A nightmare. It was impossible up here in the brilliant sunlight to imagine quite how it went.

I had read the story: about the bacillus and how it evolved in primeval mud, just one of the billions that have always truly owned this earth. A tiny slender living thing, slow growing, slow to multiply. When it was first seen by a human eye, its discoverer, Koch, even called it 'beautiful'. A little organism that made its way into human hosts directly from the earth through mouth or nose, or, 8000 or so years ago, via the bodies of cows as humans tired of walking the earth unencumbered and settled to farming. 'Take, drink,' said the big sweet-breathed creatures with their soft brown eyes, giving up the milk intended for their young. But the bacillus they had breathed into their bodies from the earth as they moved about pasture land, grazing, had no such fellow feeling. It simply spotted another likely host and swarmed aboard, settling to consumption, hollowing out cavities and creating growths sometimes compared to cheese curds, sometimes to tiny bulbs: the tubers, like little potatoes, that gave the disease one of its many names. Its work is visible in ancient bones: in the mummified remains of Pharaohs, and on the skull of a child who died thousands of years ago on the hills behind Menton. His cranial bones bear the marks of a meningeal tumour.

I've read the story of the search for a cure. The tale of oils, of herbal decoctions, of the king as magical miracle worker, touching the sufferers of scrofula — the swollen tubercular lymph nodes which resembled 'little piglets'. Another of those curiously endearing names for dread disease: little potatoes, little piglets. There's a kind of rustic intimacy in the words. There is poignancy in the diminutives, and in the desperate longing of superstitious practice. And how strange it is that Sam Johnson was taken as a four-year-old to be touched by that little pink porker of a monarch, Queen Anne! How odd that the man who became the exponent of reason, compiling his orderly dictionary, should have been touched by so primitive a practice.

I've read the story of consumption's triumph once the poor of Europe and America had been herded together into city slums so squalid that, by the middle of the nineteenth century, fully half of Britain's population is thought to have been infected. A third of the population died from it. The little potatoes had found fertile ground. It passed in the breath of lovers, from mother to child, between sailors and the inhabitants of Pacific isles. It infected people doing nothing more remarkable than renting a new home: they walked about admiring the size of the rooms and their pleasant aspect while the bacillus stirred to life beneath the floorboards, having survived for months in household dust. It enforced a ruthless equality: the factory girl tapping in her clogs to her loom before daybreak died the same gasping death as the languid musician playing nocturnes to a scented audience, the windows open to a smooth lawn and the splash of fountains. They died, objects of pity and the veneration we offer those who die young and far too thin, like those holy anorexics of earlier eras who starved themselves into sainthood, or the pallid models of our own. They became fit subjects for art and literature, their tiny hands perpetually frozen, their deaths greeted with anguish and a high B flat.

They were also good business. Sanatorium treatment — clean air, rest interspersed with moderate exercise, a rich diet — may have had no proven scientific basis, but it made luxurious international destinations of obscure mountain villages like Davos, Nordrach, Saint Moritz. In New Zealand, the sanatorium style was less ostentatious. Waipiata looks more military camp than Swiss resort. The complex is drawn up in plain ranks across the hillside, confronting the enemy.

I have also read the story of the defeat of Koch's beautiful bacillus with the discovery of the miraculous microbe, *Streptomyces griseus*, in a sample taken from an ailing chicken. It's a great story, complete with a hero — the graduate student, Al Schatz, twenty-three years old, subsisting on $40 a month, sleeping rough in the Rutgers Plant Physiology greenhouses, living on fruit and vegetables scrounged from the Agricultural Research Station, and consigned to work in the basement because his boss was terrified by the TB bacillus in his laboratory.

There's also a villain. The boss himself, Waksman, who remained safely ensconced on the third floor but stepped in to take all the credit when it rolled in. The antibiotic Streptomycin earned him a Nobel Prize and thousands of dollars in royalties until Schatz finally filed suit in 1950 and received some recognition. He continued to be the good guy, following scientific curiosity to work for the common good in Pakistan and Chile where he dedicated one of his research papers, now reproduced online, to his 'fellow scientist and friend, Salvador Allende'. Waksman merely became rich and famous.

After the chicken and the nights in the basement, the days of the sanatoria were numbered. The Swiss turned theirs into hotels for winter sports, while in New Zealand they were torn down to make room for subdivision or were taken over by other government departments. For a time, Waipiata became a place where youth went to be corrected. Now it is a Christian retreat. God took a hand. Like one of those TV presenters scouting the perfect location, he directed a North Island pastor and his wife to its purchase. Now there are families in the bungalows. A scooter lies in the grass; there's the sound of a chainsaw cutting wood in a stand of gum trees up the hill. The pastor and his wife invited us in for a cup of tea, then showed us around. The laundry with its high ceiling for drying sheets is now a chapel; the big dining hall is buzzy with adolescents horsing around where the sick once gathered for meals and Saturday night socials. Dances were popular. After all, most of the patients were young, and one side-effect of the disease was supposedly heightened sexual energy. That hectic flush that made the eyes of young tubercular women like Mansfield so brilliant, that intensity and nervous excitement that aroused writers and composers and artists, found its expression on the hillside at Waipiata in foxtrots and quicksteps and the grapevine steps of the maxina. The pastor's wife had written a book about the transformation of the complex into a Christian centre. We bought a copy. It seemed that God had attended to every detail from the moment of purchase. He had even found them soft furnishings at a very reasonable price.

Menton was a more lavish affair in its tubercular heyday — though those ornate palaces with their plaster friezes and mirrored halls would have echoed to the same cough in the night, the same feverish and giddy hope, the 'spes phthisica' noted by the physicians. That did not alter on hillside, mountain or coast.

THE BEAUTIFUL MORNING

On beautiful mornings
flowers fling up their
bright skirts, trees wink
and children run from
their parents' hands to
stand in the crack that
has opened overnight
outside the kitchen.

They jump in.
They jump out.
In and out
as if it were

a crocodile.
The earth lies still
and lets them jump
in and out
of its gaping mouth.

On beautiful mornings
the front of the bagel
shop falls down flat on
the street. The pub
slumps into the gutter
and the church lays
down its heavy cross.

It falls among the
daffodils. Fragments
no bigger than a man's
hand. The flowers
gasp. Their mouths,
their glossy lips, say
Oh.
Oh.
Oh.
What a beautiful day!

So here we are on a beautiful morning, walking up the avenue de Sospel to visit the Winter Palace. We cross the road through the public garden with its park benches and orderly ranks of scarlet flowers. We dodge more cars and begin to climb the avenue Riviera. It winds uphill between high walls. There is the sound of cicadas up here away from the traffic, and the clink of cutlery from open windows. We walk measuring the distance between slabs of shade, for the sun is intense. About us walk the wraiths in their summer voiles, their slender necks supporting straw hats ornamented with veils and flowers. They carry parasols and stop from time to time, as we do, to perch on a low wall, to catch that elusive breath.

They did not come so early in the season, of course. They did not, like those tourists spreadeagled on the beach at Garavan, come for the summer but for the winter, drawn south by a book. You can look it up on Google: every foxed and well-worn page is there. *Mentone and the Riviera as a Winter Climate*, by the English physician James Henry Bennet. From the moment of its publication in 1861 it was a bestseller, as were its successors. Bennet added to the title as his travels permitted: *Mentone, the Riviera, Corsica and Biarritz as Winter Climates* (1862) and *Winter in the South of Europe* (1865).

Reading it now, *Mentone and the Riviera as a Winter Climate* seems an odd book to become a bestseller. It kicks off with a detailed account of the region's topography, with tables of diurnal temperatures. Bennet describes the geology of Menton: the limestone that retains the summer's heat long after the winter has set in elsewhere, radiating its benevolent warmth upon the town. He describes the vegetation: the groves of lemon trees which form the basis of the region's economy, the olives and wild thyme with their tough aromatic leaves, breathing, he says — for he is a lyrical man as well as a doctor — 'all in unison like little lungs'. He mentions the brilliant light and the way the cloud comes in from the sea only as night falls, climbing the steep hills 'like a Turkish genie'. The English climate, he says, is best for invalids in the summer, but in winter the climate of Menton is to be preferred.

He goes on to compare Menton with other health destinations long considered ideal by northern Europeans, and dismisses them roundly. Naples, he says, is nothing but '500,000 dirty southerners in damp sunless streets in the midst of every abomination by which the eye or the smell can be offended'. Its evening *passeggiata* takes place along a promenade where seven sewers empty their noisome load into a filthy sea. In storms the effluvium floods the streets. And it is the fish from this vile ocean that are laid upon the table at the tourist's hotel.

The Mentonnais, by comparison, are a superior race: poor, of course. Bennet has witnessed a family of ten or twelve draw in their meagre catch of sprats with every appearance of satisfaction. But they maintain nevertheless a certain sober dignity. Unlike the careless Neapolitans, they keep the doors to their houses decently closed. Unable to graze large animals like cattle or sheep on the steep mountain terraces around the town, they are forced to husband their own manure. With some delicacy, Bennet manages to hint that the nightsoil of Menton does not therefore find its way in that slovenly Italian fashion into the harbour, but is spread productively beneath the lemon trees and the olives. There it contributes to the regional economy while decomposing rapidly and inoffensively. (In *Winter in the South of Europe* he goes into greater detail: about the trees are dug trenches where 'indescribably filthy rags' of wool or linen imported from Italy are laid, to which manure is added and the whole covered in soil.)

To his report of a modest industrious population, a sheltered location and a warm climate, Bennet, like all writers in the popular health book genre, adds his personal endorsement. He himself had visited Menton unwell, troubled and exhausted by overwork, and recovered there. He promises that others following his regime, 'walking when they are well enough in the open air, indulging in moderate activity in the optimistic company of other invalids', will, like him, find a cure.

It was expensive, and only for the wealthy, but the effect was instant. Bennet's later books suggest the area's transformation with poetic descriptions of chartered excursions by carriage or donkey to fern-fringed torrents the equal of any in Scotland where visitors might gather primroses or violets (though by 1865 the locals were charging for the violets). Handsome and picturesque young women still walk barefoot down from the mountain terraces bearing baskets of lemons on their heads; when no longer young enough to bear heavy loads, they move onto harvesting olives with equal diligence, on their hands and knees for eightpence a day. But commodious villas are already nudging the lemon groves aside. There, in 'hygienic situations' a short distance from town, those stricken with physical affliction may recline on cushions 'like an invalided lizard on his wall', exposed to the open air and healing balm of nature. Roads are being constructed, the railway is extending its reach, letters now take only thirty-six hours to travel between Menton and London. Nice has its English promenade, Monaco its slightly suspect German casino, but those places attract mere 'health loungers', rather than the genuinely ill. Those who are more serious should waste no time, but dedicate every energy to spending as much of the winter as possible in Menton. 'The most satisfactory cases of arrested and of cured phthisis I have seen have been among those who have the power and the will to return again and again.' The frontispiece hammers home the message with an engraving of a swallow and the Latin tag *Euns rediensque gaudet!* — 'Going and returning, he rejoices!'

Thousands were seduced by the swallow and the violets. The new railway carried them in comfort from the north. It also transported all the foodstuffs necessary to sustain people less inclined to survive on sprats. Good butter was brought from Milan, familiar fish species from the Atlantic coast, beef almost as good as British beef from the mountains north of Nice.

Swaying on horsehair and mahogany in their first-class compartments, the sick travelled south from London, Paris and Saint Petersburg, and the hotels went up to accommodate them. Massive structures with hundreds of rooms, surrounded by gardens of plants never before seen on this coast. You cannot help wondering what the local people, those discreet Mentonnais behind their closed doors, thought of the invasion. As an aside, Bennet mentions that historically they had been reasonably free of tuberculosis: recurrent fevers, yes, cholera, typhus. But lives spent in the open air with no fires for heating even in winter had kept the people strong. So, were they troubled by this sudden influx of coughing, spitting and death?

Other southerners similarly visited were. When George Sand and Chopin visited Majorca in 1838, the innkeeper asked them to leave as soon as he became aware of Chopin's tubercular condition. Furthermore, he insisted that Sand pay for a thorough cleaning of their room, including whitewashing the walls. They were then unable to find any local people who would help them move to the only alternative accommodation — an apartment in an uninhabited monastery. 'We could not secure any servants or any help of any kind from the local peasantry, as not even the poorest wretch wanted to work for a phthisic,' wrote Sand in a book detailing their tribulations.

That book, *Un hiver à Majorque* (*Winter in Majorca*), written in 1852, reflects an odd division that existed at the time within Europe. Around the Mediterranean — on Majorca, for example — ordinary people seemed to have had no doubt that tuberculosis was contagious. Without any knowledge of bacilli or any medical authority, they were convinced that the disease passed between individuals, even from stranger to stranger. In northern Europe, however, medical authority insisted upon hereditary weakness as the prime cause: individuals became tubercular because they had inherited a weak constitution, sometimes exacerbated by reckless living. So the Catholic south believed in an invisible but nevertheless potent agent before which all humans were rendered equally vulnerable, while the Protestant north adhered to a doctrine of individual responsibility: live moderately, avoid sexual excess, choose your procreative partner wisely, and all will be well.

What the people of Menton thought as the Winter Palace and the Riviera rose on their hillsides can only be guessed at. The poor leave no record. Their thoughts and feelings are usually the invention of well-heeled travellers, novelists and observers. The Mentonnais lived well within the zone that believed in contagion — but perhaps the offer of work overcame any natural self-protective caution. They donned the smart hotel uniforms, emptied the blood-spattered spittoons, swept up the dust, washed the plates of their smart, sick guests — and simply hoped for the best.

It was all a sham anyway. Those hotels with their gilt and Oriental fakery were indeed as flimsy as an operatic set, founded upon scientific fallacy. Possibly those little walks and optimistic diversions provided respite, but the tubercular tourist was no more likely to be cured in Menton than in London or Saint Petersburg. The air here is warm but faintly sticky, trapped within the armpit created by the muscular bulk of the Alpes-Maritimes. Humidity can reach ninety-five per cent — perfect for the growing of lemons, but fatal for anyone whose body is in the business of growing those little potatoes. The results are evident on the terrace above the town occupied by Menton's cemetery — the place de Maupassant called 'the most aristocratic cemetery in Europe'. The dead are English for the most part, though there are also plenty of Russians, Swedes, Dutch and Germans — and they are nearly all young, for tuberculosis is a disease of the young. A Polish woman, Janina Lewandowska, who died at twenty-seven in 1912, flies up in white marble from an ornate sarcophagus. William Webb Ellis who picked up the ball and ran, so inventing rugby, is there. Aubrey Beardsley is here, dead at twenty-five: a young man who with his grass-green hair — 'If I am not grotesque, I am nothing...' — wouldn't have dreamed of picking up a ball and running with it anywhere.

Mansfield isn't here, though back in 1995 visitors to the Mansfield room often assumed she was. I myself didn't work in the room. On my first day in Menton, I walked over to view it. I opened the door. It was completely enveloped in a feathery white mould. The chair, the desk, the floor were fluffy as if covered in damp feathers. Mould grew along the bookshelves and formed little cheesy curds around cracks in the ceiling. Damp was percolating down from the terrace above, the terrace where Mansfield reclined, pen in hand. The damp leached particles from the limestone plaster in the room beneath. The air was suffocating. Choking. I couldn't breathe. I shut the door, sat in the little yard coughing, and decided to work elsewhere. I set up my desk in the bedroom of the Palais Lutetia and left a note with contact directions on the gate at the Isola Bella for visitors in search of Mansfield.

To those who assumed she was buried in Menton, I said no, she's in Fontainebleau, near Paris, where she died after running up the stairs at the Gurdjieff Institute to prove how well she was after weeks sleeping above a stable, imbibing the breath of sweet dairy cows. It was an old European treatment for consumption. She had spent a few months here on the terrace, composing that vision of Menton that has become the lens through which others see it: mimosa, and orange blossom, a sweet place rendered in repeated diminutives — 'little', 'small' — that feel so like love. She wrote here of things seen or heard or smelled with all the sensuous intensity of fever. An orange, a letter, the postman ...

Whenever I read her letters or diary entries from Menton, I am reminded of flowering currant. As children, my sister and I came down with scarlet fever. It's a dimly recalled state of heat and strange dreams, blood pouring from my nose and soaking the pillow, our tongues swollen like strawberries, our skin peeling away like dry paper. And then it passed and we woke one morning to a kind of lightness. We felt cool and fresh as if we had grown new skin. We were allowed at last to get up, to walk on unfamiliar wobbly legs to the sitting room where we discovered the table set with a birthday tea. Cheerios popping from their crimson skins, a meringue cake with candles, and presents. A *Tiger Tim* annual for me, *Chatterbox* for my sister, and a doll each. My sister's doll was a baby with a knitted bonnet and smocking, and mine was a walkie talkie. A proper doll of the kind I had coveted ever since the bride doll that was a prize in a school raffle. She had fair hair in plaits, and a striped frock and little round-toed shoes, and there she was, standing on the sitting-room Feltex with her arms reaching out. You could take one of her plastic hands and walk her about the room, one stiff leg strutting after the other. If she fell she squawked Mama! Mama! from an arrangement of holes on her stomach.

We clutched our dolls and ate our cheerios in sheer amazement. How astonishing that we had been sick for so long we had forgotten our birthdays. After the meringue cake our father gathered us up, one on each arm, and took us outside. It was spring, when before we were ill it had been barren winter. The sun was warm on our new faces, and everything jittered, everything smelled of damp earth and growing. By the dunny, the flowering currant was in full spring blossom. Our father held us close so we could see it properly. The tree was dizzy with bees. Every blossom had its bee burrowing in headfirst, tiny legs wriggling in ecstasy in yellow rompers of fresh pollen.

That's what I think of when I read Mansfield describing an orange.

THE TINS

It's the little things that
break: not towers and
bridges where soft men
in hard hats pose on
rubble. It's the woman
who took her grand-
child's hand and said
don't worry, here, let's
sing about a little duck,
while her house shook.

And now she cannot
bake. The custard
squares have fallen
and the chocolate slice.
The peanut brownies
gone to dust, the afghans
crumbled and the ginger
crunch. The carrot cake
is frosted white with
toxic sludge and
underneath the sink
tins rattle. Muffin tins
and pie plates and the
12-inch tin for weddings
and Christmas.

Let's sing about a little
duck while the cake tins
rattle in their secret
empty place.

It's no longer fashionable to believe in 'spes phthisica', that special
heightened nervous creative energy gifted by tuberculosis as
some small compensation to its sufferers. Earlier commentators
were more certain of its existence. A friend has lent me a study

published in 1945 by a French critic, Vincent Le Rolle, of three tubercular artists: the painter Watteau, the symbolist poet Laforgue, and Mansfield. He identifies tuberculosis as one of the factors driving Watteau to retreat to his gilded Cythera, as the primary cause for the deep melancholy pervading the work of Laforgue and as one of the reasons for Mansfield's intense engagement with everyday reality. *'Elle vit dans une sorte d'extase perpetuelle devant la vie la baigne d'une radieuse lumière'* —'She lives in a sort of perpetual ecstasy before life bathed in radiant light.' The tough ironic stories of the *German Pension* Le Rolle dismisses as work written when Mansfield was 'not herself'. She became herself truly, he says, only when she became ill, separated from the world, the wraith on the terrace at Garavan, unable to enter a sanatorium because patients were forbidden to work and she could not bear not to be able to write. She chose the terrace though it was lonely despite her best efforts to tempt Murry south with her recitation of beautiful sensation: the mimosa, the charming fishermen, the orange blossom. A hopeful siren call designed to draw a timid husband fearful of contagion from grey old London. There she sat on the terrace that doubles as the roof of the Mansfield writers' room, like Linda Burnell reclining on her steamer chair in Wellington feeling light as a leaf and tentatively, delicately, risking love. 'Hallo, my funny,' she says to the baby lying beside her, the little being who has weakened her.

That is the Mansfield Le Rolle, in his highly perfumed fashion, prefers. There's a hint of the same slightly repellent blend of sexual fastidiousness and eroticism that created Mimì and Violetta, women rendered frail by illness, exquisite as porcelain. He does not go on to say that the bacillus itself, that slender silver rod, carries some mysterious toxin that confers creative genius, but he does say that it heightens the response in individuals already possessed of creative gifts. Tuberculosis assists an individual to become '*profondement lui-même, et le depouille du conventionelle dans lequel s'embourbe le bien pourtant*' — 'It helps the artist to become profoundly himself, as it strips away the conventions which bog down the healthy.' So, Watteau's delicate constitution from boyhood prevented him taking up the manufacture of tiles, his family's trade. It was ill health that opened the way to Paris and that strange Pierrot confronting the viewer with his melancholy white mask, and the young lovers embarking not to journey *to* the isle of love, but to *leave* it, while they are still young and in perfect beauty. It was tuberculosis that created that gorgeous farewell in which people are gathered in a city gallery taking down an artist's works and packing them away, the women turned aside, exposing their lovely slender necks and the sweep of their silken gowns: the artist's final work, unless you count the invisible ones he painted while he lay supine on his deathbed, rendered mute by disease, but brush in hand furiously painting his *poèmes paints* on the empty air above his head.

Spes phthisica. The delicate, creative, deluded hopefulness of the tubercular.

It may not be a fashionable notion. Today the language of disease is less fanciful, more military: there are 'battles' against cancer, victims 'put up a long fight', researchers are engaged in 'defeating' disease — the kind of language, in fact, that my mother used when she flung open the windows to let the fresh air in to build up our resistance. The story of the battle against tuberculosis is amazing, its results wonderful. We understand the cause, we understand its control. We know that these bacilli, these slender rods, do not actively wish us harm. They are, unlike us, too simple for deliberate malice. They are merely going about their ancient purpose, replicating themselves, creating the conditions they require for survival. But if during their sojourn in the human body the bacilli might stimulate something beautiful, that is some compensation perhaps. Perhaps it is spes phthisica you hear in the opening poem of Keats' first collection when the young poet — not yet diagnosed but probably already infected — stands tiptoe upon a little hill and

> The air was cooling, and so very still,
> That the sweet buds which with a modest pride
> Pull droopingly, in slanting curve aside,
> Their scantily leaved, and finely tapering stems,
> Had not yet lost those starry diadems
> Caught from the early sobbing of the morn.
> The clouds were pure and white as flocks new shorn
> And fresh from the clear brook; sweetly they slept
> On the blue fields of heaven, and then there crept
> A little noiseless noise among the leaves,
> Born of the very sigh that silence heaves.

Perhaps it is spes phthisica that colours Mansfield's echoing vision of Eastbourne as Eden, viewed across a vast distance of time and space and personal experience in 'At the Bay':

> Very early morning. The sun was not yet risen, and the
> whole of Crescent Bay was hidden under a white sea-mist.

The big bush-covered hills at the back were smothered.
You could not see where they ended and the paddocks and
bungalows began.... A heavy dew had fallen. The grass
was blue. Big drops hung on the bushes and just did not
fall; the silvery, fluffy toi-toi was limp on its long stalks,
and all the marigolds and the pinks in the bungalow
gardens were bowed to the earth with wetness.... Ah-
Aah! sounded the sleepy sea. And from the bush there
came the sound of little streams flowing, quickly, lightly,
slipping between the smooth stones, gushing into ferny
basins and out again; and ... something else — what
was it? — a faint stirring and shaking, the snapping of
a twig and then such silence that it seemed someone was
listening. Round the corner of Crescent Bay, between
the piled-up masses of broken rock, a flock of sheep came
pattering. They were huddled together, a small, tossing,
woolly mass, and their thin stick-like legs trotted along
quickly as if the cold and the quiet had frightened them ...

Hair loss, diarrhoea, haemorrhage — yes. But there is also that
vision of the lovers embarking on a golden afternoon from
Cythera, the autumnal melancholy of some Chopin étude, the
evocation of morning that catches at the heart and stops our
breath.

So here we are, two hopeful little humans, rather sweaty and
pink, walking up a hill in Menton to see the Winter Palace.
The air is hot and still. Cicadas saw away at the afternoon.
The road zigzags up between apartment buildings and high
walls. When cars approach we flatten ourselves against warm

stone and wait for them to sidle past. At a corner we glimpse a large and leafy garden with palm trees and creepers. Beyond its walls stand two massive buildings: the Winter Palace and the Riviera, nudging up against one another like a couple of cruise ships in too tight a berth, both jostling for a glimpse of the sea below. The buildings are so close they almost touch at one corner. When the Winter Palace went up, the owners of the Riviera which had once dominated the hillside were outraged at this flashy interloper with its snowy plaster and ornamental gilding. Now, both buildings look a little shabby, their gardens on closer inspection a little ragged. There are cars parked where carriages once turned. The elegant dining rooms, the reception rooms, the big bustling kitchens have been replaced by apartments, no doubt similar to the apartment we lived in for six months at the Palais Lutetia on the neighbouring spur.

Our apartment had high ceilings and white plastered walls, and tall narrow shutters with awkward locking devices. The walls were hung with paintings of fishing boats daubed on an azure sea. The floors were cool with a honeycomb pattern of hexagonal tiles, slippery under the pointed wooden feet of uncomfortable chairs upholstered in Provençal florals. A bowfronted sideboard stood in the lobby with gilded feet and broken handles and a drawer that contained photographs of the owner as a young woman modelling for health and beauty on the Menton foreshore in that era when the Riviera was rebranding. The bottom had fallen out of the tubercular market and the coast was selling itself as a summer destination. Our landlady wears a dashing white tennis dress and carries a racquet. The rooms in the apartment were big and airy, and at the back looked onto a steep bank covered in nasturtiums and creeping plants where tribes of wild cats ranged and squabbled by night. The air in the apartment smelled faintly of cat pee, but it was cool and welcome after the hot climb up from the market with bread and tomatoes and little round goat's cheeses coated in black ash that squeaked against your teeth. There was a small terrace where we sat to eat, keeping a wary eye on the top-floor apartment where the owner watered her plants with careless enthusiasm, the overflow splattering on the canvas of our sun umbrella. Once she dislodged a pot entirely. It smashed onto the terrace in scraps of terracotta and blood-red pelargonium.

Perhaps the apartments of the Winter Palace are more elegantly regulated. Perhaps not. We can't go inside to check. There are locks and codes to negotiate. We cannot catch a glimpse of the operatic staircase, the mirrored smoking room, the electrical elevator or the interior plasterwork of Cerutti-Maori. We stand outside, looking up at the white face of the hotel with its windows and balconies like some limestone cliff face where birds come to roost in the crevices.

Having got here, we are not quite sure why we bothered. We are hot and sticky in the afternoon sun. We stand in the car park while the wraiths of pale girls in button boots and boys in their uncomfortable collars breathe in the air around us. The walls of the Winter Palace are white, like frosting, like the wedding cake in *Great Expectations* that was all icing on the outside but consumed within. Gone to dust. There is something uncomfortable about the place, like those white sarcophagi in the Menton cemetery, that Polish girl in white marble flight above the town. How perfectly the illness suited its era, with its potential for sentimentality and science, for profit and grief. I stand in the car park thinking about Mimì and Violetta, and the hectic flush of fallen women falling faster. I am thinking about Mansfield and wondering about the impact of a bacillus: would she have written just those words had she been fit and well and left to grow old in furs, an imposing literary doyenne with a double chin, publisher of an influential literary magazine, holding court over some smart place in Kensington?

The cicadas in the ragged gardens of the Winter Palace are deafening. Clinging to dry exotic bark they saw away in that brief interval allowed them in the sunlight. Seven years below ground, then only a day or two up here in the open air to fit it all in. Courtship, mating, procreation, death. Pick me! Pick me! they call, their little legs rubbing frantically. The sound is high pitched, painful on the ear. The sound could almost be the sawing of a violin.

A man in a brown cardigan.

The sound could almost be 'Three Blind Mice'.

Or it could be the vibration of slender silvery rods, here in the shadow of the Winter Palace with its walls of white bone overlooking the shining sea.

BLACK AND WHITE

He left the camera rolling.
Black and white in Super
8. The kids on the
wharf, the collie dog,
black and white, the
man throwing black
sweets from the deck of a
white ship. The camera
shakes. The sea pulls back
from bare black sand and
the wreck of black boats.
A white line forms across
the screen. He keeps the
camera rolling. Black and
white in Super 8. The
white ship lurches like
a drunken sailor, sinks
into a black chasm as the
white line races in, bursts
in white bubbles. And he
keeps the camera rolling
as the kids go and the
dog goes and the whole
damn town goes, in black
and white.

No need for music in black
and white, nor muffled

drum. All cars in black and
white travel with wreaths
in the trunk. All the lads
jigging in rows down a
country lane have gas
masks at their shoulders
like their own staring skulls.

And that arm lifted from the
engraver's curling steel is
not waving. Plump putti
burst their cheeks as the
city blows in black and
white. But that arm was
pink, the sea was blue and
the bagel shop, remember,
was chocolate brown.

A walk to the Botanic Gardens

Dunedin, May 2010

Autumn in Dunedin. The bush on the hillside across the valley is patched with gold. Damp brown leaves are sticky underfoot. We are walking to the swings. Huia and I. I'm autumn too. Gnarled. Grey lichen hair. Leaf fall. She's spring. Two years old in pink gumboots. She has dressed herself. A green and white spotted skirt with insecure elastic. Red woollen trousers. Odd socks. Blue and white striped sweater. Her backpack — she says 'batpat' — has a stuffed woollen lamb that looks as if it is riding on her shoulders. In her hair she wears a bobble with a pink fairy.

We are walking down The Steepest Street in the World. She lives halfway up. It's too early yet for the tourists who will arrive mid-morning to walk to the top, then turn around like the nursery rhyme and walk back down again. Sometimes they roll Jaffas down The Steepest Street in the World. Sometimes they try to drive their campervans up, gunning blue smoke and cheering. It is a tourist attraction, listed in the guide books. They take photos — though the place won't look anything special when they return home. Just a street with cars and little wooden houses. They'll say, 'Where was this?' They'll say, 'What were we doing there? What day was this?' They can buy a certificate to prompt them from a building on the corner that used to be a post office until the restructurings of the nineties. The certificate says 'I walked up Baldwin Street, The Steepest Street in the World' in gilded italic. The post office too is now a tourist attraction.

Huia likes sitting on the back of the sofa in the living-room window, watching the tourists. She sits with Gus the cat as the tourists march past and the campervans groan and fart diesel. Sometimes tourists stop and take photos of her. She'll be that kid they saw — when was it now? That day they walked up this street. Where was that? A little kid with a cat. But today she is not in the window watching the tourists. She is with me and we are walking down The Steepest Street in the World.

We descend from sunshine to the cool of the valley floor and the busy road. Along the way we stop to pop fuchsia buds at number 10. Her mother has shown her how to do that, as I showed her when she was little, and my mother showed me: pinch the pink swelling bud beneath your fingers, squeeze hard. Peel back the blue petals of periwinkle flowers to find the little golden fairy toothbrush with its tip of white floss at the centre. Nip the end of a nasturtium or pineapple sage flower for the drop of honey. Blow the down from a dandelion to tell the time. Pierce the stems of daisies to make necklaces. All those pointless, pleasant things. We pop some buds. In a week or two we'll be able to make dancers from the fully open flowers, snapping off the stamens till there are only two tiny legs, then poking a stick through the green bodice of the dancer's dress to make her arms, extended in second position. We pop the buds, then she walks along the top of the wall outside the student flat with its jaunty handpainted sign above the door: The Jolly Roger, est. 1682. Triangular hillocks of beer cans are arranged on the windowsills, a sofa is crashed out on the verandah, the windows are curtained with old sheets, and there is the certainty of crusted saucepans piled in the sink, spotted knives by a hotplate, that haze of growing, of brain and body swelling, splitting, stretching, tasting, reaching, touching.

I stand by the wall holding my grand-daughter's hand so she can balance, placing one gumboot carefully in front of the other. Damp rot dimples the weatherboards of The Jolly Roger. There's a clothesline skeletal in an overgrown yard, all sagging wires and wonky arthritic arms. It's forty years since the gritty sheets and the Olivetti portable on a table made from an old door perched on a couple of trestles. Forty years since the armchair beneath the plum tree in an overgrown back yard and Dylan going round and round, a'changing, a'changing over the same crack.

What happened in the interval?

I grew up, I suppose. Got the certificates with the curly writing and the seals of red plastic imitating medieval sealing wax. Travelled to work on trains and buses in the company of other grown-ups. Earned my own money, got married, bought a car, bought a house, paid tax. Had sex several thousand times since the fumbling on those gritty sheets — in long grass and sand dunes and cars and tents and rooms. Surreptitiously in a room where a doll on the bedside table concealed tissues beneath a pink crinoline. Warily in a room in Ireland where thirteen holy pictures suggesting stern procreative purpose lined up on walls the exact colour of old tobacco. Happily in a room where a saxophone moaned twelve floors down on the city pavement and the sighs of other people drifted through the heating ducts. My body's loose now, crumpled like old knitting. It has stretched over babies, swelling till it seemed the skin must pop, but each child emerged in the usual fashion, streaked with cream and raspberry red ripples of blood. Except for one who flicked like a little fish in the dark waters within my belly. Then stopped. 'If it comes away when you're at home,' said the doctor. 'Just pop it in a bottle. I'd like to take a look.' My black olive. My son . . .

Then the babies grew and we knew what was coming because we'd read the books. There were stages, phases, an ordered sequence to their growing. First, they would smile. How good it was that the first thing they would do to mark their deliberate human-ness would be to smile! Other creatures demonstrate their essential selfhood by standing up within a few minutes of birth, ready to move with the herd. Calves wobble upright with their mother's encouragement. And lambs and foals. Piglets fight for the teat. Kittens and puppies snap and practise the kill when their eyes are barely open. But humans look up, and laugh. And then they practise leaving. They roll over to see where they might go. They drag themselves upright so they can view the wide vista of the sofa or the coffee table. They totter off toward the door or an open gate, driven by that relentless human curiosity. They run from you, laughing, and for a good while you play at running after, to gather them up and bring them back to the safe place where the game started and they can begin all over again.

So here we are on this autumn day walking down The Steepest Street in the World to the swings, because my daughter's body has stretched too and this little girl has slid into the light. I stand beside her as she walks along the wall, she in her gumboots, me in my old lady camouflage. I am Grandma. Grandmother. Granny. Nana. Tua. Nona. Baba. Dadi. Yaya. Oma. Donna. Sobo. Lola. The babble of babies. I am the Old Woman. The Little Old Lady of the jokes. The Mother-in-Law of the comic postcards. I am apple pie, I am rosy cheeks. I am baggy stockings. I am the one who is timid and overly cautious and drives at no more than 30 kilometres per hour. I am the vulnerable one easily conned by the fast-talking door-to-door salesman. I am the Mum of the Mum-and-Dad investors who can't spot a dodgy investment adviser. The silly old fool who falls for an obvious scam on the internet. I am the woman whose anger is absurd, hitting out at people with her umbrella. I am the nag, the withered hag, the shrieking harridan, the crone. In stories I compete with the hero for the loyalty of daughters, the shadowy figure who offers the alternative of running home to mother. I am the target market for creams and potions made from the urine of pregnant mares which promise to halt the process of withering. Or I might wear purple in an act of pathetic defiance, featuring as that old gal on the birthday cards as a hoot, a real laugh, with one unlikely leg in the air. Or perhaps I become peculiar, talking to the cat and forgetting to wash, the woman who once might have been tossed on the fire.

I know the Old Woman. When we were children, we threw stones on her roof on our way home from playing softball at the park. The Old Woman smelled of old socks and blue cheese. I know the rattle of stones raining down on the stink of her and her lank grey ringlets.

Repellent at worst, irrelevant at best. Barely visible in this bright morning light outside The Jolly Roger where youth is stirring in its dark cave, like those children in that Colombian tribe who were kept in darkness from birth till they were brought forth at puberty to be a reminder to all their people of the amazing dazzle of this world. Its endlessly receding horizons lying beyond any open door, any open gate. This wonderful globe that is one continuous, endless curve, rolling steadily around the sun.

Huia shakes away my hand when she has found her balance. She wants to walk along the wall by herself, arms spread for equilibrium, but I stay close, being autumnal and therefore anxious. Someone who has slipped many times and fallen: on damp moss, and mud and ice, and once on a slice of boiled carrot. Someone who has hit her head on cupboard doors and lintels and rocks and tarmac. Jammed her fingers in car doors, hit her elbow, strained her back lifting a television, had prickles in her skin and under her nails. Tumbled headlong over park railings, and down steps and over her own shoes. Someone who has barely escaped annihilation on narrow country roads and, entering a roundabout, who was nearly bowled by a Volkswagen one dark night in Heidelberg — which would at least have had a certain touristic appropriateness. Someone who has eaten contaminated seafood and dodgy chicken and eggs seething with toxins, who has eaten berries but so far they have all been good berries. And mushrooms but so far they have been good mushrooms. Someone who has flown in planes with problematic landing gear and unspecified mechanical failures but so far she has never sat next to the weak spot, been sucked through a hole in the fuselage at 30,000 feet. Someone who has gone to sleep with a candle burning but not woken to howling flame and choking smoke and a melted telephone. Someone who has walked unharmed through dry grass infested with venomous creatures whose bite or sting could kill in seconds. Someone who has absorbed countless billions of bacteria and viruses, some lethal: scarlet fever, measles, TB, cancer . . . And lived.

But I have seen the pictures. I know people whose car swerved at the wrong second, people who have gone down to despair and jumped, people who have lost sensation in their feet, then their arms, then their tongues and minds. I have known a man who took a plane to a convention one morning, a good man, a kind man: he flew into the walls of a slender city tower and now he dies, over and over, on the television screen.

So when Huia walks along the low wall in front of The Jolly Roger est. 1682, I hover ready to reach out should she stumble and fall, because I know it can happen. Cars swish past on damp tarmac, and down the road near the supermarket there is some business of orange barricades, warning lights, a road crew at work. Huia walks steadily, plump with confidence, along the wall and jumps (I hold her hand for this part) neatly to the ground.

We walk on past the house with the sleeping cat on the sofa on the verandah. It opens one yellow eye. Huia says, 'Hello cat!'

She is not entirely sure she is not a cat herself. She is not quite sure where being a cat ends and being a human being begins. She crawls sometimes like a cat. She licks milk out of a saucer like a cat. It is conceivable still for her that she might grow to be a cat, curling on a warm cushion to sleep. Equally, she might become a dog. She speaks to dogs as if they understand and might say hullo in reply. She thinks she still has a choice, as if all those billions of exchanges of DNA, all that fumbling and sighing, that stretching of skin, that bursting forth into the light, that growing and withering and dying, might be rolled back to a point where there could be a choice. She might have evolved not as one of those near-hairless bi-pedal creatures with its big crinkled brain like a walnut in the bowl of her skull, but as dog, or cat, or bird. On her human feet clad in gumboots, she splashes through a puddle. The latest in a long line of walking people.

All those walking feet . . .

LIPSTICK

Marge ran out in her
pyjamas. But that's no
way to end: crumpled
in faded pastel,
barefoot, pinned to

the earth by the
clothesline's scrawny
cuddle.

She climbs back into
the shaky dark, finds
her fluffy jersey, the
one everyone says
brings out the blue
in her eyes. Her fine
wool trousers.
Italian leather shoes.

And lipstick.

A dash of crimson.

Thick enough to leave
its mark on any saviour,
should one come
knocking,
kissing her
awake,

in her tomb of
shattered glass.

My mother had small feet. Size three. She walked quickly, with a slight slide on the right foot: tap shht tap shht, in high heels. You could tell it was her coming down the street: that rapid nurse's gait, always running late, always catching up, rushing home with some mince in a bloody package, late with putting on the tea.

My father's gait was more deliberate. He was a stocky man, who had done boxing in his youth and played rugby. There was a photo of him lined up with his team. They had their arms folded fiercely, giving nothing away, and their hair was sleeked flat to the skull. We wore his little velvet Athies cap with its golden tassel for dressing up. On Friday nights, when we walked back up the hill from town, my sister sat in the pushchair, jammed in by groceries and library books, while my father gave me an elephant ride. I sat on his shoulders, keeping a tight grip on two hanks of hair sticky with Brylcreem. I could look over the fences into gardens where roses stood tiptoe in a ballet froth of gypsophila. I could see through windows lit in early evening into rooms where people sat around a table or in their easy chairs being private and not noticing as I swayed past, ducking to avoid the branches of trees overhanging the footpath as my father walked steadily uphill.

He liked walking. He could not bear to be cooped in an office. He worked as a meter reader, walking up and down every street in Oamaru, finding out what lay behind every fence in every yard. Knowing the houses to avoid for their fierce dogs or because lonely old ladies lay in wait with their offers of tea while cats slept on the table among packets of stale biscuits and unwashed dishes. This walking seemed a continuation of the war when he had marched about that flat black-and-white place we knew from the photos stored in a shoebox in the sideboard. The place was Egypt, where palm trees grew, like the ones on the brass plate that hung above the mantelpiece. There was a brass dagger on the mantelpiece, and an ebony box with mysterious little pictures made of bone: birds, a sphinx, a pair of legs without a body on top, a big eye. They were not pictures but actual words, if only we knew how to read them. In this strange place, our father had worn baggy shorts and sported a rakish moustache that made him look fierce and piratical and not like our father at all. He said the moustache was red while his hair was black, which sounded very peculiar. They marched a lot, once nearly into a wall when a sergeant major, new to the game, froze and was prompted into action only when one of the men yelled, 'Say something, Sarge! Even if it's only goodbye!' When they had practised enough, they all marched to Alamein where my father was injured. Shrapnel peppered his body, leaving only a forefinger and the twisted stump of a thumb on one hand. When we were older and too big for elephant rides, my sister and I squabbled over who should hold that hand when we were walking back up the hill from town. We didn't like holding The Bad Hand. We wanted only to hold The Good Hand.

When I was about twelve, the walking stopped entirely. My father's knees began to swell. His hands twisted till he could barely hold a pen or turn the pages of a book. His face swelled. The soles of his feet became unbearably tender. The cause was uncertain. It was perhaps an inherited condition. There had been a great-aunt back in Scotland who had some unspecified condition that left her bedbound. 'She could only move her eyelids,' our mother said. How terrifying! Imagine not being able to do anything except blink!

Another possible cause for our father's state lay under his skin, in those tiny shards of shrapnel that sometimes worked their way out through his damaged hand. We stood entranced to watch him tug them forth with a pair of tweezers beneath a strong light. So tiny, those pieces of the war. Tiny, yet perhaps powerfully toxic. He groaned with the effort of turning a page, lighting a cigarette, lifting a teacup. The walking came to an end. There could be no more meter reading, opening the gates on all the mysterious gardens of Oamaru. Instead, he was forced to work in an office, though he had his desk as close as he could manage to an open window. And eventually, when even that became impossible, the walk from car park to desk a marathon march with callipers and crutches, he retreated to bed, where he read about people walking through Africa in search of the Nile's source, or racing by motorbike along the Silk Route to China, or sailing on flimsy craft across wide oceans in the wake of Brendan or Kupe. People moving about in the wide free open air.

Behind him and my mother were other walkers: a great-great-grandfather who pushed a barrow over the Kilmog to fetch sugar and flour from Dunedin; the grim line-up in the Pioneer Gallery who walked away from bare Highland hills to take a ship to a place where they could elect their own minister unimpeded by some landowner, and sing their doleful psalms, all ninety-four verses, without interruption. And there were the nameless hordes on my father's side, the Irish paupers who walked the green lanes carrying nothing but a spade for employment, the women noted by nineteenth century tourists who took to the road with four or five raggy children at foot.

Maybe this restless lineage is why I too get impatient when trapped in car or plane, why I am only truly comfortable when outside, moving about in the open air. Some gene, nested on some chromosome, makes me twitchy at confinement. I have to step out the door, feel my heart settle to that lovely primal duple beat. My dreams at night are of walking across hilltops, my nightmares of being lost in strange buildings with increasingly narrow rooms. In real life, I dislike malls and internal access routes made up of corridors and stairs, like the plywood maze that is Heathrow. Under stress, I'm a runner. I have friends who burrow into bed to recoup, the duvet over their head, but I am consumed by the impulse to flee, to find open air. Both my daughters as babies escaped on a regular basis, crawling under hedges, heading off on purposeful infant journeys of exploration pushing a pram with a teddy and a biscuit. In adulthood, they stride through their lives, down past the zoo and along the city streets, through the Botanic Gardens, around the waterfront. One walked round Annapurna on a whim with a girl she had met on the plane to Bangkok: no plan, no special clothing. They wore enormous woollen sweaters purchased from locals along the way. (The girl later married a local and took him back to Ireland. She hoped for a mountain life, but he preferred Rosslare.) My younger daughter spent a long summer walking the whole length of the South Island from Farewell Spit to Fiordland along the spine of the Main Divide. Through forests and alpine valleys, across snowfields and shingle slips, and a river in flood that lifted her, although she was heavily laden, and bounced her about like a bubble before depositing her safely on the opposite bank.

Every morning, I go for a walk. The routine begins on waking. I lie in the half light in the hypnagogic half state when thoughts still flow through the random channels carved by dreams. It is the best time for knowing what will come next in the book I am working on, or for realising with absolute certainty that I have made an error. Got a date wrong. Changed a character's name or hair colour — errors I had not even been thinking of when I lay down to sleep the night before. But there they are in the morning, clear and unmistakable as I lie looking up at the ceiling and the spider who lives in the light fitting as if it were a little round yurt slung upside down on the endless steppe of Flat White.

There is always the sound of the sea, either pitpat on summer sand, or thrumming like some massive machine, the air filled with agitation and the smell of seaweed and the depths of the ocean. That same salty smell that lies between your own toes, in the twist of your own navel, in all your crevices. There is also the sound of birds. Kereru stripping the almond outside the window of all its leaves and all its fruit. Their big blue bodies crash onto branches too light and whippy for their weight, and sway wildly. The birds gobble and emit small guttural moans of satisfaction. Oooh. Oooh. There is the sound of sheep and cattle and the rasp of our neighbour's farm bike, the joy of dogs released to run, ears flat, tongues lolling. Grubby larrikin dogs. If they could choose, they'd drive souped-up cars with loud exhausts and booming stereos. They'd wear tatts and beanie hats and lean out windows yelling cheerful obscenities. They race the farm bike FUCKFUCKFUCK across the flat and off up the hill while I wake, think, get up, cold feet on lino, flick on the kettle, shower, dress. I go out and feed the chickens. If I'm late, they fly up and nip my legs in a manner that leaves no doubt that they are indeed the descendants of dinosaurs and that if I were to collapse and die in the chicken coop I'd be picked clean in a matter of minutes. My terms of compliance are eggs. Smooth. White. In their declivity of straw.

I gather the eggs, put them in their basket on the bench. A cup of tea. A piece of toast. Then I put on my boots and walk to the waterfall.

THE TABLE

She sits under the table
crosslegged between
four stout legs.
Victorian legs in tight
gaiters, poised on
polished toes. Outside,
her pots glissade and
the glasses are spin
drift. The roof cracks.
The cat ran through

the flap and has not
come back.

She sits in the dark
on the rough side of
Sunday. The wood is
bare down here, torn
from a tree. She gets
her woolly hat. The
table is saw scrawl
screw and scratch.
She brings a cushion
and some crackers.
The table is a bare
bivvy. Brace and
bruised knuckle.

She flings a sheet
over. She will
live here
for ever.

I arrived in this valley one night with a man I had met at a poetry
reading in Akaroa: Blenheimer in plastic cups and twenty-seven
poets. I was recently divorced, living on my own for the first time
in twenty-five years. I had a writing residency, scribbling away at

a novel in someone else's room at the university. Her toothbrush and tissues were in the top drawer of the desk. Her books lined the walls, great slabs of nineteenth-century fiction interspersed with pre-Raphaelite posters, all big chins and curly hair. Lizzy Siddal floated, catching her death of cold in a flower-strewn bath tub above my desk. Lizzy, whose copper-coloured hair grew so luxuriously after death that it crammed her coffin: a fact discovered when the artist Rossetti had her dug up seven years after interment so he could retrieve the poems he had in a sentimental moment tucked in beside her for the afterlife. At my borrowed desk with my borrowed view of the concrete walls of the music block, I felt deeply temporary.

The novel I was writing was my second. The first had been written two years earlier in a strange restless state. After twenty-five years of marriage, I had found myself dreaming about a small house in which I lived alone. It had paintings on the walls and a fire in the grate: a house that was, and yet was not quite, the home I had known as a child. It was smaller than the cavernous villa in which I was raised. It was cosier. No one was throwing teacups at their loved ones. The dream house had none of the tension of living with other people. It became compulsive, a secret existence I imagined as I lay in bed before anyone else was awake. The dream house had in the back yard fruit trees I had selected myself. They had lovely names: Peasgood Nonesuch. Cox's Orange Pippin. Beauty of Bath. It had roses over the verandah. They were lush and old-fashioned. Their names too were beautiful: Gloire de Dijon. Souvenir de Malmaison. Albertine. The flowers were short lived but exquisite while they lasted, and nothing lasted for ever.

It was in this state that I began a novel. It was about two girls. One was dutiful and engaged with the world. She grew up to have work and family and political opinions and social obligations. Her sister was mute, her silence masking subversion. She did not care about other people or their opinions, nor did she possess a sense of duty. I wrote early in the mornings. I stopped lying in bed and crept instead to a downstairs room with a sturdy Redstone computer and massive printer with long rolls of continuous paper that sometimes jammed or flopped to the floor in a muddle. I wrote huddled in my dressing gown, until I had to get dressed and go off to work. I was teaching high-school students. Boys like young steers whose knees nudged aside the spindly broken-legged desks with their scribbled graffiti and intricate sketches of genitalia. Girls who chattered and didn't see the point of reading *The Outsiders*. I didn't either.

'What's it for?' they said as I handed out the worksheets: tick the boxes, yes or no. 'Why do we have to do this?' The girl who couldn't read but could yodel like an Opry star. The girl who told me about her mum's friend who had just flopped it out and it was, you know, ENORMOUS. The sullen long-haired girl who had to leave at fifteen to marry, have children, serve the Lord. The beautiful boy who fell on his head helping his dad paint the garage roof. The trickster who took a rotisserie chicken from his bag to nibble as he filled in the worksheet, yes/no.

Before I encountered them all for another day, I sat in the quiet room with no sound but the steady click of keys as words formed orderly lines across a bare white sheet. It was cold at the back of the house. The heater purred ineffectually. My back hurt. My fingers were chilled. I wrote without a plan, with no theme, no plot outline, ignoring all the rules I was teaching by day. And when it was finished and the two girls came together as old women in an apocalyptic future, sharing a bed in the ruins of the Oamaru post office, something had changed in me too. In the novel, as the sisters reunite, rain begins to fall on land that has been dry and dead. The world is sweet, set once more for renewal and rebirth. And I was no longer married. It was over.

I left home with a typewriter and a painting by Lindsay Crooks and my bike, and moved south, back to the island where I had been born. Nor'westers ripping strips off gum trees, the Alps ruling off the plains with a clean white line, and those little southern towns that had set out with such ambitions — all Victoria Squares and plans for universities, and seaside esplanades — then shrunk. The butcher shop is boarded up, the post office is a craft shop, the land reserved for the esplanade has been claimed back by a rampant ocean. And there is no sign of a school, let alone a university.

I came to Christchurch ill prepared for life alone, even if it was to be in a cottage with apple trees and roses. I had decided on the plane as I flew away from twenty-five years, rising up over the plain of Manawatu with its graffiti squiggle of creeks and toetoe, that I would be brave from now on. I had spent too much of my life being timid. I feared flying, for instance. And swimming in deep water. And arguments. But no more. I would do everything I feared, all at once. I would learn to swim properly in water too deep to put my foot down. I would travel alone. I would say yes and have adventures rather than backing off into caution and saying no.

So when a man I had met briefly at a poetry reading asked if I would like to come out to the Peninsula for the weekend, I said yes. I saw him waiting outside the Four Square as the bus pulled in. Woolly jersey. Corduroy trousers. And those green gumboots English people wear in the country. The kind Princess Diana wore when she was young and sufficiently in love to trail about in tweed watching Charles kill wildlife. In a dusty Cortina we drove up into the hills behind Akaroa. The road zigzagged up the crater wall. There was a dull gleam of water in the flooded caldera that formed the long harbour far below. A skinny moon skidded about between clouds, and as we neared the crest, tussocks tossed their hair in a sharp wind. There were patches of snow in crevices. We bounced onto gravel, skidding into corners as we followed the road round many turns downhill. Bush elbowed in on either side. The road levelled. We slowed for a ford. Then we went through a gate and stopped. Outside, the air was cold. It was like diving into an icy South Island river, and dark in that deep velvety fashion that is so startling after life in the city. A creek ran somewhere nearby. Stars were thick as daisies overhead, their glitter just enough to see by. I followed the shadow of the man through long deep grass. He opened a door.

A housebus. A small room with a wood stove burning, 'Popsicle Toes' on the stereo, a curry cooking, books and prints around the walls. It felt deeply familiar. It was Ratty's house in that picture in *The Wind in the Willows* where the little animals sit snug on a winter evening on the riverbank.

I have lived in this valley ever since. A few months after we met, we bought the old farmhouse down by the beach with its rattling wooden frame and warren of busy rabbits under the kitchen floor. The farmer had built something more convenient in Summerhill stone up on the hillside. The house had been neglected for some years. Floorboards could give out unexpectedly. There was the brush and squeak of other inhabitants in walls and ceiling, objecting to disturbance. But we cleaned and painted and mended, and it became accommodation for walkers on a coastal track. Every night from October to the end of April, people walk around the headland and follow the farm track down into the bay. They stay the night, then walk away next morning through the bush of Hinewai Reserve to Akaroa on the other side of the hill. Along with the house we acquired three acres, the rabbits, an orchard of apple trees, a hen house and a pig pen. The place was built a hundred years ago by the farmer's great-grandfather: a sullen Frenchman called François who arrived here back in the 1850s and called the farm Renegat. His valley was reputedly a haven for runaways for whom its inaccessibility was a decided advantage. The easiest access for many years was by sea.

The house stands at the head of a narrow bay walled by towering cliffs of basalt striped crimson with deposits of volcanic ash and frilly white from centuries of bird droppings. Geologically, it is a 'pocket bay' typical of this peninsula: a deep indentation on the flanks of a near-circular ancient volcano. So our house is the small thing that you might find in the lining of a pocket: a peppermint perhaps. A ten-cent piece. It stands alone by the little sandy beach, a flimsy thing built to a design better suited to warmer climates — Queensland, for instance — with verandahs to keep out the sun, high ceilings, and a kitchen on the southern side at the end of a long passageway that channels a refreshing draft. In storms it creaks like a ship at anchor. The roof is a kettledrum beneath winter hail.

The valley rises steeply behind between twin lava flows laid down like leonine paws upon the southern ocean. In summer each headland is nibbled to golden stubble by sheep. The house lies at its breast like the cartouche on the breast of a great recumbent Sphynx. Each year the sea reclaims another few centimetres, exposing black verticals of charcoal and burnt pipi shells in the clay. Before us, there were aeons when this valley was an intricate mass of bush and birdsong. Then a few centuries of people. They built a pa on the hillside, and kumara gardens where we grow apple trees and silverbeet. Their tools emerge from time to time from the soil, like the past pushing its way through living skin. Pounamu patiently fashioned to cut or dig. A massive adze rose one day among the stones near our neighbour's tractor shed. Tools laid aside or perhaps hurriedly concealed when the pa was sacked and burned three centuries ago, Ngai Tahu coming down upon Ngati Mamoe. There are stories of a mere being dangled over a cliff to test the alertness of the local people, and of an early morning raid in fog so thick that one of the invaders attacked a standing stone, thinking it was a sentry. And of a man running for his life around the headland and of his pursuers pausing to observe the courtesies of who should deliver the death blow. The pa was sacked and the place on the hillside called Parakakariki, 'bird scrape', referring to the earth that is torn up by little green parrots — kakariki — when contesting territory. So, by metaphorical extension, the earth that is left torn and bloody after human conflict.

Fires were lit on the beach where we lie sometimes on warm nights to watch the traffic passing overhead: the falling stars, the little chugging beams of satellites circling the earth, taking all our photographs. When our neighbour was a boy, there were long sand dunes studded with skulls and human bone, but they were all torn away during the storm that sank the *Wahine*.

Every morning I walk away from the beach and the small white house, up the valley to the waterfall. Past the sheep yards and the gum trees with their gargling cargoes of magpies and tui. Across the creek on the wooden bridge, looking always to see if there are eels unfurling like steel ribbon. The ones I see are always young and slender, but once on the beach we saw an eel as big as my leg nosing her way across the sand where the creek fans out to meet the ocean. A big old female on her way to the tropical waters round Tonga, along the path she followed a hundred years ago when she was no more than a prickle of broken glass, a tiny shard of living, swept south by ocean currents over thousands of kilometres to this creek, in this valley. For a hundred years she had lived in her dark pool, long before our neighbour slid down the sand dunes among the skulls and bones, long before we drove down the road in a rattling Cortina. We had no idea of her existence, but there she was, while the forest on the hillsides was burned and cleared, and cows arrived, and sheep. Head on to the current through flood and drought, waiting while the males left as they do when they are mere striplings, no more than thirty or forty years old. They headed out for tropical waters, while she stayed, growing bigger, stronger, until something changed. Some scent in the water, perhaps. Some signal from the moon. She stopped eating, her guts shrivelled and her ovaries swelled to fill the cavity. Her skull changed shape, becoming leaner and more purposeful. The pigment around her eyes darkened. And then, obedient to some other signal, one night she turned and began to swim at last downstream with the current. Past the flimsy bridge, the cows on the flat, the farmer's new brick house, our white cottage. One heavy grey muscle undulating in the tobacco-brown waters of the creek. The water is shallow where it meets the sea, too shallow for swimming. She heaved herself onto the sand, and that is where we saw her, wriggling ponderously toward the ocean. Off along her miraculous path to breed at last in warm water, in one explosive seeding. Then to drift empty, to die ...

I cross the creek where she had spent her quiet life, and enter the walnut grove. The trees are huge and spreading. In winter their limbs are skeletal like an old man's twisted limbs, but in spring they bear small posies of copper-coloured leaves. Clumps of white narcissi scent the air. In summer each leaf is an open hand, and the nuts are round and green. We pick them and prick them with a needle and make a dark and resinous liqueur. In autumn the nuts fall. They litter the ground among knobs of sheep shit, and crack underfoot. We gather them too, those tiny crinkled brains within their perfect shells. The leaves turn golden and the sun takes longer each morning to filter through, snagging on small protuberances on the hill crest. Light forms great aureoles along the skyline before the earth rolls over a fraction. Down here on the valley floor the light under the walnuts becomes dappled and damp.

The Frenchman, grumpy François, planted the trees after he arrived here, washed ashore by currents of war and chance. He married a young woman who lived in the valley, and inherited the farm when her father died up on the hillside coming home from Akaroa after a few days' hard drinking. Magee and a mate called Woodhams had set off from the pub with a few bottles of spirits for sustenance along the way. Over the next day and night they meandered homeward through dense bush as the weather turned to snow and hail. An unseasonable change, for it was early October, but the hills here rise in an abrupt volcanic syncline from the sea to 700 metres — the same height as Mount Cook village — and snow frequently powders the tops. For us, it is no more than an inconvenience, a day or two perhaps without power. We read by the stove, go to bed by candlelight with a sensation that this is a little old-fashioned, pleasantly romantic. It's a brief interruption, a gentle time without intrusion from the outside world — no phone, no email, no television. But then we are not drunkenly trying to find our way through dense bush in 1854. It took Woodhams another full day to make it down to safety. Magee's body was not found till three weeks later, in 'an advanced state of decomposition' in a creek. The coroner's verdict was accidental death, but local legend preferred something more dramatic. That part of the valley is called familiarly — though not on any map — Murderer's Gully.

The incident is recorded in the *Lyttelton Times* of 1 November 1854 in the leisurely style beloved by nineteenth-century journalists. The rest of the page is taken up by a lengthy account of a chimney fire in Lyttelton ('Every assistance was eagerly rendered by the inhabitants to arrest the progress of the flames ...'). And by a speech by a local dignitary devoted to the vexed topic of how colonists might get their hands on the oh-so-desirable 'Waste Lands' currently occupied in their careless fashion by obstructive natives.

News is a more hurried business now, a palimpsest of Yahoo!-sized bytes: *Crews battle fire. Business confidence slips. All Blacks triumphant. Baby joy for Celine.* But as I walk up the valley beneath the walnut trees, that is what I find myself thinking about. Twigs and scraps of the stories we call 'news'.

THE PLUMBER

The plumber knocks at
the ground three times
with a steel bar.
Knock.
Knock.
Knock.
Asphalt cracks and water
bubbles up and clay and
old pipe laid down when
old boots tramped this
way from the Carlton
on the corner. Old muck

bubbles at our feet
like closing time and
pissing on a bush.
Knock.
Knock.
Knock.
Like a man asking for
attention in a crowded
place. Time he says
behind the bar. It's time.
Knock.
Knock.
Knock.
Everybody must find
their way home now.
Drink your last drink.
Sing your final song.
Knock.
Knock.
Knock.
'See there,' says the
plumber. 'That's the
break.' The earth
smells sour, stale
breath from a
cracked lip.

Time.

It's time.

Once I too wanted to write news. I wanted to be a journalist like Randy Stone on the radio, who covered the night beat for the *Daily*: there were a thousand stories on the mean streets of the dark city. Beautiful troubled young women approached him with tales of woe, incompetent cops missed the clues, corrupt administrators at city hall barred his way. But Randy got his story, and when it was filed, and bad had gone down at last to the forces of order and good government, he called for a cup of coffee. Of course he required a restorative shot of Bushell's Coffee and Chicory Essence after all that danger and high tension. I was almost a teenager before I realised he was actually calling 'Copy, boy!', sending off that week's story to feature as the headline in the morning edition.

Journalism seemed an exciting career, though as a counter to Randy there was the only journalist I actually knew, Uncle Leo, who wrote the racing page for the *Oamaru Mail*. He did not seem at all glamorous. He smoked rollies, wore a felt hat glued to the back of his head, and kept the stub of a pencil behind one ear for ringing sure bets. Maybe it was the hat that put me off, or the fact that newspapers in the sixties liked their tyro reporters fresh from school before they had developed high-falutin' ideas. I wanted to go to university. I wanted to study English. English was novels and poetry and plays. I was good at English.

I liked acting. I had been Marie-Antoinette in disguise in a one-act-play festival, wearing a cottonwool wig and a gown hired from the Operatic Society. It was sewn from shot silk, the kind that changes colour from green to red to purple and is used to line coats. It smelled, it had to be admitted, of someone else's sweat, and required safety pins to fit properly, but I adored the swish of it. The bodice was corseted so that my breasts — 32A and generally unremarkable (no boys ever stared or muttered about overshoulderboulderholders as they did to girls more amply endowed) — were pushed into a startling décolletage that made me self-conscious and thrilled all at once. I adored the sweet scent of the sticks of greasepaint and the little red dot that was placed with great delicacy on the end of a toothpick at the inner corner of each eye.

'There,' said the typing teacher who was doing our make-up. 'That will make your eyes brighter!'

I blinked into the mirror behind the stage at the Opera House. It was ringed with bare bulbs, and in their glare my eyes did indeed look brighter. I adored that, as I adored the gasp — slight but unmistakable — when the aged crone stood upright and revealed herself to be the Queen.

We didn't win. The boys from St Kevin's had done a play about people on a train, in heavy mittel European accents. But there had been that intake of breath from a darkened auditorium, and at that moment I would definitely have chosen to become an actress rather than a journalist had I known how to do that. But in 1963 there was no drama school, no obvious doorway into the profession. I knew no one who acted. There was the Operatic Society: *Oklahoma* in gingham skirts, *South*

Pacific in naval white, Noël Coward in brittle English accents looking for a pee-ah-noh, a pee-ah-noh, yes a pee-ah-noh. But to join them seemed impossible. The people who acted in the Operatic Society — the man from the florist's, the lawyer's wife, the woman who drove a red sports car — were so dauntingly self-assured. They sounded English and lived in the two-storey houses we called 'doctors' houses'; the women wore lipstick and smoked in public, not rollies like Uncle Leo, but little black Sobranies. The gasp from the auditorium was not enough to blow me across that divide.

I liked poems too. When I was little I wrote poems and sent them to the Children's Page in my mother's *Woman's Weekly*. You won stars, and when you had enough stars you received a book: hardback books with black-and-white illustrations of children in boarding schools having midnight feasts. I longed to eat chocolate in a dorm, risking the wrath of Mam'selle. I wrote stories too, and one, a long story in chapters, I was permitted to read aloud to my standard four class on Friday mornings. It concerned the adventures of four children at a boarding school who encountered smugglers. I wrote it in an exercise book I had covered with the embossed wallpaper my father used to decorate the sitting room. I loved writing that story, finding out what happened each week. I loved it as much as folding the wallpaper carefully to make a perfect mitre corner.

At high school, life became more serious. I was in 3P1. P for Professional. The girls in 3P2 would become nurses and primary-school teachers. In 3C for Commercial they would work in offices and do typing. In 3H for Homecraft — well, who knew? Housewives, probably. Making bacon and egg pies on a farm, or pushing a couple of fractious kids to the shops in their slippers. But the girls in 3P1 were destined for higher things. They did Latin and would go to university. With a few exceptions they were the first generation in their respective families to be so privileged. They were the chosen ones. They had been blessed with The Opportunity. They would read *Cranford* and Jane Austen. They would become familiar with the habits of the rural gentry of nineteenth-century England. They would read Milton and Donne and *Hamlet*.

3P1 was not a place for smugglers, and boarding school no longer looked quite so appealing anyway. There were boarders at Waitaki. They were called 'rats'. Daygirls were called 'scabs'. The boarders kept to themselves and had puzzling internecine quarrels. They marched to church in town on Sundays two by two, and wore black velvet dresses with white lace collars for best, and one weekend one of them plucked out all her eyebrows and eyelashes and was sent home looking odd and bald because she could not stop crying. At Waitaki, I wrote poems for the school magazine, generally in sonnet form:

> *I too have met the deer and know their ways.*
> *Their horns have threatened me, their red eyes gaze,*
> *Still, from darkened corners . . .*

I wrote an essay for a competition that every year commemorated that glorious moment when Oamaru stepped onto the world stage as the place from which, in 1913, news of Scott's failure to reach the Pole was telegraphed. An oak tree at the end of Arun Street also remembered it: the death of Scott and his men in that terrible little tent, defeated by the unsporting dog-eating Amundsen. The topic was 'My Visit to Antarctica' for which I received a large dull book called *Heroes of Nowadays* as a prize. The heroes were all like Scott: admirals and fighter pilots, and someone called Freddie Spencer Chapman who at first glance appeared to be no more than an ordinary English school master but who had spent years fighting the Japanese in the jungles of Burma.

My essay was total fantasy anyway. I could think of nowhere I would less like to visit. Ice, snow, no trees, and those men with their bleeding lips, the one who got up and said he'd be gone some time ... I much preferred frocks and bonnets and the silly sister who ran off with an officer and the sensible one who got the nicest and richest young man in the end.

So literature seemed the perfect choice when at last I was free to take up The Opportunity at Otago. All that free milk had been for this. And all that free healthcare, the polio vaccine in its little paper cup that meant I would not spend my life in an iron lung, just my head and feet exposed and a book propped on a rack in front of me for sole distraction. All those free trips to the murder house where my teeth were drilled and the cottonwool bumblebee slung on a piece of dental floss was scant reward for not wriggling. All that education that had been freely mine from the moment I encountered the dress-up box at kindergarten till the moment I graduated and arrived, in cap and gown, neatly framed next to an arrangement of plastic gladioli on top of the television. In my hand, the rolled diploma that guaranteed the glowing future.

I remember this girl as I stand with my grand-daughter outside The Jolly Roger est. 1682 on a cool autumn day. I remember her in her yellow mini-dress and knee boots walking down these same damp Dunedin streets to lectures. Her hair is long and straight. I remember the swing of it and the knock of some heavy book in the bag over her shoulder. There is no time now for poems and stories. She writes serious essays on Lawrence and Wordsworth and Eliot, big serious men who wrote big serious books, booming from the literary high ground. Though even then the high ground was coming under siege. The girls in the mini-dresses were preparing to sap the redoubt.

On the surface, of course, nothing appeared to be happening. It is always so difficult to tell what is going on in a reader's mind. A curious stillness pervades all those paintings of women reading. Those virgins and saints tilting the book toward the celestial beam, those Parisian street girls sprawled on uncomfortable settees, seemingly unaware of the painter and that they are stark naked, so absorbed are they in their book. Those Dutch women standing at windows, reading. Women seated out of doors in flowery gardens, reading. Women lying among opulent cushions, reading. So impassive. So inscrutable. So private. So deeply personal. Who knows what might be going on in their minds? The reader could at one remove be experiencing the thrill of illicit passion or considering bloody rebellion. No wonder the dictators and leaders of cults burn books and issue their edicts of forbidden texts.

But as Carol Hanisch put it — or maybe it was Shulamith Firestone or maybe Robin Morgan, one of those sappers back in 1969: THE PERSONAL IS POLITICAL. The young woman in her miniskirt had been blessed with opportunity. She had been educated. She could earn her own money. She could take a pill that prevented conception. She might marry, but then again she might not. She might have children, or she might not. She might keep her own name, or change it to something she liked better, like Tree or Sky. And when she had a free moment — on the train to work, at night on the sofa — she wanted to read books and poems that reflected her reality. She wanted to read *about* women like herself. She wanted to read books *by* women like herself. She insisted that there was a difference.

In books written by women, the heroine would no longer be an isolate, separated from family and friends like a single sheep separated out from her flock by that wily dog, the hero. Juliet would have her gaggle of friends, just as Romeo had his. In women's books, the heroine would not live beautiful and solitary before dying young. Nor would she grow from beautiful beloved to dutiful Lawrentian mum, plodding out at dawn to stoke the range and fill the snap tin. Women's heroines had jobs: that lab bench mentioned by Virginia Woolf, or in an office, or a catering business. They had friends and families, whom they abandoned sometimes for life in a cottage in the woods and pleasant self-sufficiency. They had a social context. They menstruated, they had sex, sometimes bloody and brutal, sometimes ecstatic. Sometimes just for fun. The camera lens would look up at the man's face, watching him writhe and grimace in orgasm, rather than looking down at the woman beneath. Women in women's books fell in love, selecting a man from the herd as they had always previously been chosen. They had affairs and veered off the moral path and got away with it. They no longer sidled off to an upstairs room to give birth while the hero paced the floor to the accompaniment of offstage shrieking. Birth was described in all its swelling cramping detail, soaring on waves of pain to the explosive, ecstatic release of delivery. Breasts oozed milk. Women's heroines raised children and led chaotic lives in messy kitchens with baked beans glued to unwashed saucepans.

The books were dismissed, of course, almost immediately, with that instinct for the rhyming taunt we all learned back in the playground. 'Aga sagas.' Precursor to the equally dismissive 'chick lit' with its sparkly nineties universe of high heels, a PR job in the city and lots of delicious wine. But I remember how they seemed to the young woman who once inhabited my skin: they were fantasy, but they felt like a kind of fact. She absorbed their versions of love and marriage and adultery. She observed how their heroines decorated their houses with country prints and large kitchen tables, and how they named their offspring: Olivia. Noah. Poppy. There were English models and there were American models which were darker and more intense and featured women who had wild sex with Laingian analysts or moved from dull suburban marriages to communes in Upper New York State.

She read these books as if she were taking notes. Moreover, she learned from the Australian feminist Dale Spender that she was not alone in this. For women, Spender wrote, novels have always had an educative function. The form evolved in parallel with modern science at a time when men were energetically sailing from Europe to discover the world and creating hypotheses to test reality. But while men like Banks were sailing to the Pacific, recording the plants and observing the canoe that emerged from a narrow bay on an island named Banks in his honour, and noting the native who stood in it, riding the uneasy ocean with assurance — women back in England were equally consumed by curiosity. Confined within the home, they marshalled data and experimented on a smaller scale. They developed a new art form, the novel, the perfect medium for the examination of hypotheses about human behaviour, the perfect medium for travelling widely within an imagined universe. For women, fiction has always been much more than mere distraction.

So the young woman was not alone. She learned from novels as much as she learned from the analysts: the loud clever ones like Germaine Greer who used to stand, a friend told her, on the tables in the uni cafeteria at Sydney to conduct vigorous debates. And the quieter reflective ones like Virginia Woolf, carefully defining how money and a decent meal at midday make such a difference to human perception. The glorious repast of quail and delicate confectionery at the well-endowed men's college contrasted with the stew and prunes at the brave but impoverished women's college.

I remember the young woman who once was me reading these things. I remember her standing in the stacks at the University of Toronto where she went to study drama after Otago, and how amazed she was by the dusty row of Aphra Behn's plays and novellas. How astonishing that this person had written so much, that there was not merely a gaping void before Jane Austen. Here were all these novellas and plays with their casual Restoration licentiousness; here was this brutal account of a slave insurrection in South America. How extraordinary that this woman had written these things and made her living on Grub Street. How could she have been so thoroughly forgotten? And she was only one of an immense press of forgotten women, ridiculed, ignored, plagiarised, burned, legally deprived of property and independence. Once you began looking closely, the world past and present was crammed with insult. How appalling that her own grandmother had been considered unfit to vote, cast in with the mentally subnormal. How insulting that entire issues of *Landfall* in the fifties and sixties featured not a single woman poet. How bizarre that it had been Dorothy Wordsworth who wrote:

> *For oft, when on my couch I lie*
> *In vacant or in pensive mood,*
> *They flash upon that inward eye*
> *Which is the bliss of solitude.*

Which were of course the best lines, the ones she had always felt were strangely too feminine for William, striding about the hills on his long legs in all weathers.

Feminist writers mentioned a 'click', an instant of intimate recognition, a sudden understanding of how the world operated and how you as an individual had been living within that world and adapting to it. For the young woman who was me, life became a barrage of clicks. She seemed to live against a constant background hum of irritation and indignation, like some appliance with a pilot light ready to burst into flame at the slightest touch.

And the touches were slight. Tiny shards that pierced the skin, yet were too small to explain adequately. I remember her standing at a conference of English teachers to object to a movie that was being shown as a possible teaching resource. She had a job lecturing at a teachers' college in Palmerston North, a clean job, the kind you get when you have been given The Opportunity. She had two daughters, a chaotic kitchen with baked beans glued to a saucepan, and a cat sleeping on the washing, and she had a job. She liked her job. When she had a late miscarriage one year, she sat up in bed at the hospital marking exams while she waited for the little black twig that was her son to slip from the crevice onto the white sheet. The marking, the job, was all that was keeping her from screaming and running out the door into the wide open air.

I remember her standing at the conference trying to explain that this movie was a male fantasy even though it had a cast of women and it had been made really well, but by a male writer and a male director and that mattered because . . . ummm . . . well, women don't have access to the popular media and it's like Shulamith Firestone says: women never get access to the most powerful places, and whenever they do join in any numbers, well, it's a sure sign that the real nexus of power has moved elsewhere. Like in politics, for instance, governments are nearly all men and if that changes and you start getting women prime ministers, well, that's because the real power lies somewhere else, like in big business. Take art, for example: back in the sixteenth and seventeenth centuries when painting was powerful and prestigious in Europe, women were pretty much excluded and now there are heaps of women artists but that's because art isn't important any more, it's just a fringe thing, and theatre's the same. There are women dramatists and directors but today the real power is here in movies and TV, and women just don't get access, they never get to tell their own stories and instead you get movies like this one, that look like they're about women but they're not really... Her voice trails away. She sits down. It wasn't exactly being part of the Sydney Push, declaiming from a table top.

It was so easy to feel petty, but it was the petty things that irritated. The big things — witch burnings or the fight for suffrage — were obvious: who wouldn't find the killing of whole villages of women a bit unfair? But why were you making such a fuss because the bank manager looked at your husband and never once at you when you were discussing the mortgage?

I don't feel nostalgia for this irritable young woman, nor for her era. She was quite hard to live with. I remember her fondly, with slight embarrassment, as one remembers a distant cousin. She wore platform shoes and an all-in-one brown suit that made her look like a World War II fighter pilot. She had big hair, curls even for a while. She made muesli for the children and yoghurt in a preserving jar. She experimented with international cuisine. Her daughters poked at their squid sambal and said, 'What's this?'

I remember her sitting in a room at the library in Palmerston North at a new kind of event, a book festival. The room was filled with women like herself, with jobs and children and yoghurt on the kitchen bench. They had come to hear authors speak about their books. Dale Spender. Barbara Trapido. How astonishing it was to be able to listen to a living writer, to see the person whose photo was on the dust jacket. To be able to say, 'She's older/ younger/sounds different/has a better haircut/is more forceful/ more timid than I expected.' Then queuing to buy a book and have it signed, as you once collected autographs. *Roses are red, violets are blue . . .*

Then her father died. She was thirty-five and she wrote a poem, her first since the sonnets of adolescence. It was about the time her kitten died. They had always had kittens when she was a child, half-wild creatures tamed with milk and tempting morsels of jellymeat. They were never very satisfactory pets, being prone to bad temper, and often sickly with runny eyes. There was one, Blackball, a black-and-white kitten named after the lollies they bought at Woolworths on Friday night. It died. She found its little body by the flowering currant, stiff and sodden in the rain. It was sad. Her sister cried. But somehow she couldn't. She cried for imaginary deaths readily enough: children or ponies dying in a book could reduce her to sobs. Sometimes she cried for no reason, because everything had simply become too much and crying was the only option. She would sit in front of the wardrobe mirror and cry, watching with a kind of curiosity how her face changed colour to crimson and how her mouth stretched so you could see right inside to the tonsil thing at the back. And when she had finished crying, gasped the last gasp and squeezed out the final tear, she lay on her bed wrapped in her eiderdown feeling a deep relief, a pleasant empty floating. But the little kitten was too serious for crying. It was so wet, so cold, so stiff. Its eyes were not quite closed and the pupils looked milky. She sat at the table for tea that night feeling cold, her throat tight as if she had a furball herself. Her sister sat opposite, red-eyed and weepy for the loss of Blackball who wasn't even her kitten. Her father was critical. 'Why don't you cry?' he said. And all she could do was shrug. She could not explain the cold fur and the sheer deadness of being dead. She knew she was failing him. Her sister was behaving appropriately while her silence was all wrong. But there it was.

And when her father died, she was the same. Simply cold. Too cold for crying.

So she wrote a poem about the kitten and the furball of tears, and the little fantail that flew into the kitchen on the day her father died and flitted about doing silly little tricks on the curtains and lampshade. Such a pretty cheerful creature making light news of death.

The poem held it all. She had forgotten how satisfying it was to make those short lines on the rectangle of plain white paper.

One afternoon between classes she was working on it in her office at the teachers' college, adding a comma, altering a word, removing the comma . . . She shared the room with a woman named Stanley. (She had been named after an uncle who died in the war: 'Could have been worse,' she said. 'Ronald, say, or Bertrude.') Stanley was old — at least fifty — with grey hair in a bun and sharp blue eyes. She had written a book, a history of the

Waihi miners' strike in which a striker, Fred Evans, was booted to death behind the Union Hall by strikebreakers recruited by the government from the country's prisons to go in and sort the socialists out. The newspapers of the day were ecstatic when the strike ended. The *Weekly News* ran a cartoon captioned 'Rout of the Red Feds!' while the *Herald* celebrated the defeat of a 'Tyranny of Shrieking Red Socialists'. Stanley was a socialist, though not especially given to shrieking. She had gone to Waihi and interviewed people who remembered how it had felt to live history: a man who as a child had ridden his pony round town delivering the *Maoriland Worker*; another who recalled being piggybacked through the bush to Paeroa one night when his parents were forced to run from the mob surrounding their house. Then Stanley wrote a book. She made it seem simple. 'If we don't write about these things,' she said, 'who will?' There had to be a record of events other than the version in the *Herald*. The book was published. There was a launch by the white plinth that marks Fred Evans's grave at Waikaraka.

As Stanley scrambled to her desk in the little overcrowded office, she glanced at the poem about the kitten. She read it. She said, 'That's good. You should publish that.' It seemed so simple.

The poem was published in *Landfall*, and the young woman who was me tried a play. It was based on the Waihi strike, a musical for her drama students, with multiple roles and white face, like Joan Littlewood's *Oh, What a Lovely War!* She wrote a story for a competition in the *Evening Standard* and won a book token with which she bought a dictionary and a decent atlas. She wrote more stories, another play . . .

At the end of the year she lost her job. She was made redundant. Stanley too. In fact, most of the women on the staff lost their jobs because they were part-time, like her, juggling families, trying to maintain a balance. Only half a dozen women remained on a staff of sixty. The government was making economies. It all seems unremarkable now: restructuring, downsizing, staff cuts. But in 1982 it came as a shock to the recipients of the free milk, the dental care and The Opportunity, busy learning Latin for a lifetime of professional security.

Another click. A system, political or economic, could simply flick you aside and carry on, indifferent. And where were you as an individual in all this choppy water?

She was shaken. She became prone to fits of panic: sitting at the hairdresser's one afternoon, she was consumed by the urge to run that had first threatened to overwhelm her the year before as she waited for her little black twig son to have his dry birth. What if she began to scream, right here, right now? What if her mind broke, cracked up like a porcelain cup? What if . . . ? Her skin began to prickle; the sound of the hairdresser chatting about her plans for the weekend, the snip of the scissors round her ears, became intolerable. She plucked at the cape, barely able to breathe, made up some rapid unlikely story — a child needing to be picked up from school, she'd forgotten all about it, she had to go, sorry . . . Her hair was wet and uneven. She finished it as best she could in the hall mirror once she was home again, and safe.

But then the panic began to spread. It oozed out into the spaces in supermarkets and in cinemas, onto the street, into the corridors of the high school where she eventually found another job. She told no one. She took to avoiding supermarkets, shopping in smaller places where the door was never far away. She felt herself shrinking in an increasingly constricted world.

The only safe place was the page. That plain white sheet required nothing of her. On the page she was still in control. There, she could regain that simple childhood absorption in making something as perfect as a mitre corner. On the page she could write her poems and plays and stories, constructing an existence impervious to authority. No one there could make her redundant. She could do and say whatever she wanted. To begin with, she was nervous that she might be embarking on something risky. After all, life as a writer had proved tough for other women. Virginia Woolf had killed herself even with a room at her own disposal. Sylvia Plath had turned on the gas. Robin Hyde likewise. They were famous, but she could scarcely bear to read their work lest their disease somehow transfer itself from the page and rise up like some foul vapour from the poisoned Bible in a Websterian tragedy. She wanted to write, but not end up with her head in the oven in her dishevelled kitchen or floating face down in a river as the pondweed closed over.

Well, she didn't. She wrote and was published, and eventually the panic receded. She had talked about it to a therapist, a woman called Enid who had a clinic behind a Skyline garage in Roslyn. Enid took her hands and said, 'Now, on your left hand, place the version of your self whom you like the least. And on the right — your stronger hand — the self you like best.' On the left, unbidden, stood a ten-year-old girl in a pallid pastel dress, barelegged, her hair in an ugly bob. On the right stood the woman who wrote and directed plays, a woman in knee boots and a brown parachute suit, happy at a cast party after everything has gone perfectly and she's whooping it up with people she has fallen in love with, every one of them, they are all going to be her lifelong friends, and she's dancing, and the play was terrific . . . She had looked at these two versions of herself and known without a doubt that it was the timid creature in the pallid frock who wrote the poems and the plays and the stories, and that the confident self in the boots was a bit of a bore, really: good fun, but limited. So the panic with its insistent whiny 'What if?' was the reverse of that calm white page. It was the silver sixpence she had to pay for being able to write. Nothing came without complications. She simply had to learn to live with it and be, in a way, grateful for it.

THE JOKE

It's all a bit of a joke, innit?
Standup. A laugh. Here
we were on solid ground
making light of our
existence. *A man walked
into a woman walked into
a bar walked into a . . . .*
We were unshakeable.

Not easily rattled. We
were well grounded,
earthed, firm on both
feet. *There was an
Irishman, a mother-in-
law, a shaggy dog...*
We knew how that went,
here on terra firma,
well balanced, on a
strong foundation.

So were we ever surprised
when the joke came tickling
teetackatacka at the window
frame, and dwang and soffit
broke up, purling and joist
fell about and
BOOM BOOM
There's the punchline.
*And a bar walked into
a man, and the mother-
in-law said help help
and the dog, well,
anyone seen that dog?*
BOOM BOOM.

You could have knocked us
sideways. You could have
knocked us over with
a single funny feather.

So here I am, alive and writing in another era, an era more attuned perhaps to journalism than to novels, plays and poetry. Reality rules on prime time, even if it is surreptitiously edited to conform to fictional models: human beings are nipped and tucked to create a clearer silhouette than is possible in real life. Events are recounted with greater tension, and the reverses, climaxes and resolution of story, rather than the random detail of life as it is lived. News broadcasts talk of bringing us 'stories' rather than facts. And at the literary festivals that have evolved from those women's book festivals in provincial libraries, it is the journalists and non-fiction writers who draw the biggest crowds: Robert Fisk, Simon Schama, Richard Dawkins. Fiction too seems to thrive when it is 'about' something — the travels of Richard Burton, the dropping of the atomic bomb on Nagasaki, the court of Henry VIII — or based on some topical outrage. A high-school massacre, child prostitution in Delhi. Then the questions flow easily. The audience has the satisfying sensation of learning something, of encountering reality.

I enjoy that sensation too, but a few years ago I heard a French Canadian writer speaking at the Vancouver Festival. Or rather, not speaking. He sat in agony, head in hands, forced to answer questions in English, a language he clearly found uncomfortable. He squirmed, mute, through most of the session, before bursting out with, 'Beauty! Why does no one speak about *beauty*! Because that is what this is all about!'

And he was right. Beauty. The pleasure of crafting something as perfect as the mitre corner.

But perhaps I am out of step, with my grey hair, my slack skin. A few years ago, when I was in Ireland on a writing residency, I came across the Old Woman of Beare. I was supposed to be writing a novel, but I had become distracted by the old Irish texts in the Cork City Library. Not the originals, of course, which are held in a library in Dublin, all hushed and polished in a substantial eighteenth-century building round the corner from Trinity College where crowds queue to view the Book of Kells: those lovely spotlit pages with their imagery of curly-haired saints seated among tangles of gilt like rare birds in a blackberry thicket. I loved their little bare feet and the way the ankle bones are delineated, and the way they turn their feet outward in first position like dancers about to spring into action.

The Royal Irish Academy Library is a quieter affair. The doorman is cheerful in that ex-Forces fashion, and shows you where to hang your coat. The reading room has rows of shelves and a big plain table where a few people sit reading. In the far corner there is a little cabinet covered with a strip of upholstery fabric. The librarian folds it back, and there is one of Ireland's old books with its buckled parchment, its cram of words written with a feather in black ink made from the oak gall. Books that were treasured, exchanged in ransom deals, or carried around a battlefield in a gold casket to render it sacred before battle. You cannot be sure which book it will be when you make your visit: it could be the book known as the Speckled Book, or the Yellow Book, or the Black Book. Each book is named simply for the colour of its binding. Nor which page you might encounter. Some are illustrated with pictures of those little dancing saints, but most are just words. The librarians turn the pages regularly. The books are lovely, curious, ancient things.

The Cork library is less reverent. The reading room is filled with the sort of people you find in reading rooms everywhere: in winter, the old guys who sit on the streets in summer come in to read the papers out of the chill wind. There are school kids doing their projects and giggling surreptitiously behind the shelving. There are the natives of a dozen different countries dealing with officialdom on the library computers.

And there on a shelf was the old woman of Beare. We'd come into Cork to do some shopping: fish and organic leeks from the English Market across the road. The stalls of the English Market are covered. The Irish Market once lay out in the open, on the streets and quays. Old photos show piles of chairs and baskets and coal, supervised by tough-looking shawlies driving a hard bargain among a rabble of barefoot children and men in caps and lumpy jackets. I was in out of the cold myself. The wind was piercing, though the guide books kept mentioning the Gulf Stream and its ameliorating effect on the south and west of Ireland. Why, palms grow in Bantry Bay! The cold was damp, not like the bright blue blast of a Canterbury winter. It rose from the ground, penetrating your boots no matter how many socks you wore. It left the streets dark and gleaming as if they had flooded overnight. It smelled like Dunedin, of damp stone and hops from the brewery and the salt lick of the sea. No wonder the beardie men with their unkempt hair chose the reading room, sitting by the window like a bunch of old saints, flicking the pages of the *Echo*.

I was there in the warm, browsing the shelves. I like that word: 'browsing'. Like a cow picking its way from one delicious clump of clover to another. It's a drifty word, full of purposeless pleasure. I was browsing, taking down this, scanning that, keeping out of the cold till it was decent to go over to Butler's for coffee and a chocolate. And there she was, the old woman, in a *Golden Treasury*.

She was the speaker in a long poem, the oldest poem composed in Irish. She was grey haired. She was blind and she was living alone by a wild sea. She was sitting there in the dark, listening to the crash of waves and the suck as they drew back. Ebb and flow. I knew what she meant by that: the regular breath of the sea, the duple beat that is the fundamental beat of living. In the old woman's poem, it sounds as if there is a storm brewing, and there is nothing like a heavy sea to make you feel small and impermanent. The old woman does not say so explicitly, but tradition places her on the Beara Peninsula, which is pretty much like the peninsula on which I live. It has the same rounded bulk jutting out into a broad and limitless ocean, the same big bare-knuckled hills, the same moody waves beating at its shore.

The poem begins with an odd detail: the old woman has begun to bleed again. In some publications this detail is omitted, but really it has to be present for the poem to make any sense at all. It is the stain that prompted her to speak. Not 'pick up her pen'. The work is too early for that. It was copied down in the tenth century but was clearly composed much earlier, in the fifth or sixth century, when the old religion of Ireland was being displaced by Christianity. For four or five centuries these words were remembered, passed from mouth to mouth before a monk recorded them, using the new technology of ink on parchment.

That in itself seems a little odd, given the nature of the words. It begins with the blood. Today the old woman would no doubt be whipped off for a scan and some HRT — but for this woman the blood is strangely hopeful. If her body can bleed again, long after menses have ceased, could time itself go into reverse? That is what the poem proposes: that the sea could deposit stones on the shore rather than dragging them away, that she could be young once more, and powerful as she once was as a priestess in the old religion, driving her own chariot about the wide plains, the confidante of kings, beloved by young men. Now she is powerless before this new faith and its omniscient God. The work is a lament, and it is the blood that starts the keening.

Not noble blood. Not the heroic kind that is spilled on a battlefield and commemorated with scarlet poppies on Anzac Day, but the sneaky blood that makes young women wary of pale fabrics and white sofas. The kind you remember at its first appearance: you are playing French cricket with your cousins who are arguing over whether the tennis ball hit above or below the knee. You have felt queasy all morning, with a strange cramping sensation as if you have eaten something stale. Your cousin is chucking the bat at his brother and saying he won't play any more, which is a disaster as he owns the bat; he got it for Christmas, it's a real bat with a rubber grip. That's when you feel something trickling on your leg.

Your auntie is not worried at all. She hugs you and says, 'So you've got your Granny!' as if it is perfectly normal and not horrible. She gives you a cup of tea and a malt biscuit, and you sit with her at the kitchen table, listening to *Portia Faces Life* and watching your cousins who seem so childish through the window between you, squabbling over a cricket bat. You feel separate and secret and uncomfortable on a bulky pad pinned to your knickers, and you wish with all your heart that it would stop. Later, when you are much older and it is okay to talk about such things, a friend tells you she had assumed just that: you had one lot of blood and that was that. You were now able to have a baby. The news that the blood would be, from then on, a monthly phenomenon till she was old, till she was practically dead, came as a devastating shock. It was so unfair!

That is the blood the old woman poured into the well-wrought vessel of her poem as churchmen poured the issue of saints into crystal vials to act as objects of veneration. She poured blood and heartfelt regret into verses carefully crafted round an A-B-C-B rhyming scheme. I can't read the Irish, but I can tell by looking at the shape of the words that it rhymes, and translators normally render it in four-line stanzas.

Standing there in the Cork City Library, I felt another of those clicks of recognition. The click carried across time and space in those magical lines and circles we make on a bare white page. It is not that I have ever wished time to go into reverse. I don't want to be the young woman in the mini-dress. The present is far too full of pleasures like watching my grand-daughter walk along a low wall in her gumboots. But in the old woman's lament I recognised that sensation of slipping out of step with the time, stepping aside from the long procession, to sit here by the sea writing my poems and stories, scribble scribble scribble.

Other women deal with this sensation of ageing more vigorously. Dale Spender, for instance, has abandoned writing books altogether for the internet and the power of new technologies. 'Why would I write a book?' she said in a recent interview. But maybe I have too much Irish lineage for that. I'm drawn to lost causes and the beauty of the doomed romantic gesture that is the stuff of poetry.

THE POEM THAT IS LIKE A CITY

This poem is like a city. It is full of words.
Doing words. And being words. And words
that compare one thing to another thing
and words that hold everything together.
This poem has a high rise at its centre
with a view across the plains to the hills.

It has a CBD and CEOs and a thousand
acronyms whirring like wheels. This
poem is going places. It also has small
prepositions where people pause, drink
coffee and read the paper. They go to
and from and sit before and behind.
They walk across the park, crunching
like gerunds on white gravel while
watching dogs splashing. Ducks quack
and rise. Like inflections? At the end of
phrases? The way we do here? This
poem is a crowded street where words
clatter in several languages and every
thing you see or touch has many names.
This poem is written in the gold leaf of
faith and in the red capitals of SALE
and BUY NOW and all the people walk
among the words as if they were trees
and ornament and would never fall off
the edges of their white page.

This poem jolts at the caesura and all
the words slide sideways, slip from
the beam in dusty slabs. The children
who were learning how to say hello
tap goodbye goodbye in all their
voices, reaching in the dark for the
mother tongue. There is no word in
English for this. No word in any
city.

This poem is palimpsest, scraped
clean each morning and dumped
in the harbour. But at night it rises.
The moon buttons back the dark on
tower block, mall and steeple. Cars
boom hollow on a phantom avenue,
cups fill with froth and nothing and
an empty bus wheezes up Colombo
Street. Stops for the children who
perch, waiting like similes for
chatter and flight, tapping their
abbreviations.

Ths pm is lk
a brkn cty
all its wds r
smshd to
syllbls.

Each syllbl
a brck.

Autres temps, autres moeurs. 'Femininity' in the magazines
now references a pre-feminist fifties world of frocks and retro
lampshades and recipes for tea parties with china and tiny

cupcakes with your girlfriends. All the fiddle my generation cast aside for rushing off to work and the Playcentre committee and organising women's book festivals. Our food aimed for gritty peasant authenticity, modelled on the menus of French and Italian farmhouses. It went along with the wooden bench and the array of copper jelly moulds our mothers had thrown out in favour of easy-care Formica and plastic. We aspired to life in a peasant village — minus the inbreeding, of course. A kind of Hobbit world of communities, small and intimate, even in the midst of urban sprawl. Our supermarkets edged toward the farmyard, with woven baskets and straw and canned country-and-western music. The young men favoured hip-hugging velvet and frills, and their hair was long and lustrous. We said no to war and yes to flowers in the muzzle of a gun.

One morning not long ago I flew into Wellington for a meeting. The concourse sported rows of cardboard figures: an avenue of enormous All Blacks between which we walked to collect our bags from the carousel. It reminded me of visiting the British Museum and walking between those statues of lions and huge hieratic beasts that once lined the route to the palaces of potentates. It reminded me of visiting St Peter's and walking past columns whose foundations loomed above my head. It is not a sensation I enjoy. I didn't like the look of those All Blacks with their massive arms and bulging thighs, that same look that appealed to the sculptors who decorated the Reichstag back in 1939 with statues of *Übermensch* striding purposefully forward, hands clenched. The most curious feature of such figures, I always find, is how small their heads are and how insignificant their genitals, reduced to tiny plum-like clusters between those massive thighs. These figures don't think. They don't have any generative function. They are simply overpoweringly strong.

That was the year I noticed everything had become bigger. Much bigger. We went to buy a barbecue, just something simple on which to cook a few sausages or chops during summer. Once we'd managed with a table-top hibachi, then with a larger device on spindly legs. Now barbecues lined the aisles, lids raised on dials and grills large enough to accommodate an ox. Cars became big, and houses were the size of art galleries furnished with sofas so fat and inflated your feet could barely touch the floor. Politics swelled. The division into smaller units favoured by my generation — the communities and neighbourhoods — were displaced by amalgamation: cities would conflate to form supercities, a word that sounds absurd and comic book to me. The supercity, home to supermen who will not wear velvet, nor have long hair. They will shave their heads and favour the look of the assassin, the loner, the pitiless renegade.

It's a masculinist era. We are like those caged salmon who change their sex with the addition of a pinch of hormone. One minute feminised, the next masculinised. Altered by the water in which we swim and live our lives.

So I write my stories and poems in a little hut by the sea in this masculinist era. And I plan to keep doing that till something or other prevents me. Blindness, perhaps, like the Old Woman of Beare. It runs in the family. My mother became near blind in old age. An aunt, several of her cousins. Or perhaps it will be paralysis, the same disorder that overwhelmed my father. When

I was twenty-two, still that young woman in the mini-dress, a specialist in Oxford told me I had inherited the condition. I lay on a narrow gurney at the Radcliffe, surveyed by the specialist and a mildly curious group of medical students in white coats with self-conscious stethoscopes slung about their necks. I had not expected the students. Some of the boys looked quite nice, but I had on waist-high grey knickers and an old bra with a safety pin holding the strap. I lay there pink with embarrassment as the specialist outlined how I would most likely develop the condition. What was he talking about? Callipers? Reading all night in bed, groaning as I lit another cigarette, the whisper of pages turning in a silent house? Barely able to walk as far as the sitting room? The students looked down at genetically interesting me, and I wished I'd worn a different bra.

But for now I write. And before I write each morning I walk up to the waterfall. Out the gate and across the farm François inherited from his dead — maybe murdered — father-in-law back in 1854. Beneath the walnuts and the little hump in the long grass that marks the place where four of François's children lie buried. His wife, Mary, bore eighteen. In the photos she looks sturdy, like a small cob pony, with a determined chin.

Over the stile where the air shrills in late summer with the sound of cicadas clinging to the rough bark of the willows by the creek. In the swampy places there are pukeko speaking their language of click and shriek, and quails, whole families rushing about, the adults in front looking flustered as they run for cover, the chicks behind, so unbelievably tiny, running so fast that they levitate. They crash off into the dry grass. The path winds now into a reserve where the paddocks François so laboriously cleared are already on their way back to kanuka, mahoe, fuchsia. Past the place in the creek where we pick watercress, and up the track to where water tumbles over a slab of black lava.

And the truth is that now I hardly notice any of it. The walnut leaves, the cicadas, the creek. My feet move automatically every morning, stepping over each familiar root or stone. My body simply wheels me along while I think. I think about the book I'm writing, but equally often I think about news. I walk each morning with a chatter of facts and the headlines that wash in over the hill with the radio, the television or the moment I switch on email. I think about the headlines — Celine's baby joy, the failure of another finance company — and I think about the manner of their reporting. I walk through beauty, fretting about journalism and composing irritable letters to the editor. Dear Sir, how long will we tolerate storytelling and celebrity tittle-tattle as a substitute for news in this country? And what's all this with John Key and Picton the kitten/John Key finding his long-lost brother in London/John Key off to Afghanistan with twenty-five handpicked journalists, none from Radio New Zealand — too independent perhaps — to have his photo taken shaking hands with an American general? Where's the analysis of policy? How can we operate in a democracy when the critical commentary is marginalised to the blogs where people may write well but without the scope, the reach, the influence of the big dailies, and why do magazines concern themselves only with obesity and mortgages while this country blunders on to increasing inequality, a milk-powder republic led by a bland rich guy like all those bland rich guys — the ones that look like boiled eggs in suits — and why has this country abandoned the policies and systems — the free healthcare, the free education — that gave me and my generation The Opportunity, why should those same policies not work for our children and our children's children? Yours sincerely, Outraged of Otanerito.

The only time I lay all this aside is when I stop at the water's edge. The waterfall drops into a pond at its base, sometimes choppy, churned up after heavy rain. More often it is still and dark, overhung by fuchsias with their peeling golden bark. I pause there, and, for some reason, I pray. I have no idea who I might be addressing. Certainly not the God I once addressed as I laid me down to sleep, lining up all my family for their nightly blessings. Nor that Gentle Jesus who inhabited a heaven I imagined, because of the pictures in my Children's Bible, to bear a strong resemblance to the azalea dell at the Oamaru Botanic Gardens. I haven't been inside a church since I encountered the commandant of Auschwitz at thirteen. But habit is a powerful thing, and as I stand by the waterfall each morning I forget the irksome headlines, I stop being Outraged of Otanerito. For a few minutes I am just an old, deeply inconsistent woman in a woolly hat, thinking about all the people she loves most and wishing them well.

Then, puffing a bit by now, I climb the steep track up to the road where the gravel slips under my shoes as I walk back down the valley toward the white house by the sea. And the book returns, and the headlines and the business of the day.

But when I walk with Huia it is different. If she were with me on the way to the waterfall, we would stop to look at the eels in the creek, and perhaps draw them forth from their hiding places under the banks with scraps of hardboiled egg. We'd watch them undulating in their silvery skins in the dark water. We would stop to pick up walnuts in season, just a few for our pockets. We would poke our fingers in the holes on the track where the cicadas have emerged for their little life in the sunshine. In shady places there might be a hint of frost. A slight crackle to the tips of the grass. One morning the whole path will glitter. It will look like broken glass. But it is actually cicada wings, hundreds of them, shed at the moment of death. If my grand-daughter were with me then, we'd stop and she'd pick them up with her small precise fingers. We'd examine the web of veins and the iridescent blue spot in the lower corner. We'd see how beautiful they are.

That is how it is this morning in Dunedin as we walk together to the swings. It will take ages. Only a few blocks, but there is just so much to see. There is the wall to walk along, the cat sleeping in the sun, and at the intersection a truck and lights flickering, and orange cones set out to divert the traffic. Some men are digging up a water main. Water gushes up and floods the gutter. We stop to examine this phenomenon. And as we watch, a man rises up from a hole in the ground. He's a big man, heavy set, with his hard hat perched on the back of his head. Huia is entranced. 'Man coming up!' she says. And I see it suddenly as she sees it: the strangeness of a man rising from a hole where solid ground has broken open. A man has risen from that dark place under the earth into the bright day!

But then the crossing lights beep and we remember where we are headed. The swings are just across the road in the Gardens. Swings and a slide and ducks. And a fluffy at the kiosk for her and a coffee for me before we start walking in that slow meandering fashion back to her home halfway up The Steepest Street in the World. Her mum is there, and her dad, and her baby sister, Ngaio, who can't walk yet but is beginning to crawl. Rocking back and forth on hands and knees like a toy car, brrrmmm brrrmmm, building up for forward motion by gaining traction on the sitting-room carpet. The little green walking man is beeping. The lights at this corner change quickly. There is not a lot of time to cross. Cars are waiting, idling on either side.

'Hold my hand,' I say to Huia, 'while we cross the road.'

Hold my hand and you will be safe. She is still little enough to trust such simple truths. Hold my hand and no harm can come to you. She takes my hand, that lovely familiar slightly sticky little hand in my bigger hand, and we cross between the cars to the other side. And then she runs ahead, released, through the big iron gates, plump and pink with her batpat bobbing. She is just beginning to discover the world and the words that name the world. The words she'll need to explain how the world is for her, the words to say what she has to say.

And her whole life stretches ahead, like a long green grassy path, where she can walk.

JULIA AT TAI TAPU

Whenas in silks my Julia goes,
Then, then, methinks, how sweetly flows
That liquefaction of her clothes.

Next when I cast mine eyes and see
That brave vibration each way free;
O how that glittering taketh me!
    — Robert Herrick

The paddock too is clad in silt
Fine grained, it falls as white as milk.
Like rain it shimmers, falling over
Ryegrass, cocksfoot, sweet white clover.

Swamp and rivers we'd thought dead
Rise, torchlit, clad in glittering thread.
And, sibilant, high fountains play
Where Holsteins browse in naked day,

And Julia glides about her park,
A strange vibration in the dark.

A walk on shaky ground

Christchurch, September 2010/February 2011

The first was a jolt from sleeping.

We were in town that night, staying in the little flat I had bought when my mother died and we sold her house in Dunedin. It was one of a block of four built during the war from sturdy weatherboard with a concrete tiled roof and tiny gardens at the rear. We planted roses in ours, and espaliered a cherry tree along one fence because I don't really see the point of planting trees in a garden that don't bear fruit. It was intended as an investment: a rental property, a sensible option for two people who never save a penny.

In the event it was never rented. I stayed there when I was working late in town and could not face the long drive home to Otanerito. We stayed there for film festivals and parties and in the depths of the winter when the road at home was muddy or blocked by slips and the sun took hours to filter down to the valley floor. Friends stayed there, people who were between flats or working in the city temporarily. My daughter and her partner stayed there. They worked on the offshore islands, on Raoul, and Maude, and with the kakapo team on Codfish: a month on, two weeks off. The flat filled with climbing ropes and crampons; snowboards and surfboards tumbled from the wardrobes. When they had a baby she was born in the upstairs bedroom, sliding into a hot summer day as a nor'wester tore at the leaves of the trees across the road in Hagley Park. And two years later her sister was born there too, delivered in a paddling pool in the living room, wrapped in the caul like a surprising little package.

The place was rough and furnished with odds and ends: a couple of old armchairs from the garage, a second-hand bed. But gradually we did it up: new kitchen cupboards, a new bath, a gas fire. Over the winter in 2010 we painted it from top to bottom: a soft green in bathroom and kitchen, milky white elsewhere. It was pleasant work, the two of us painting while the radio played and the cold rain fell. And finally, one night in September, we were finished. We rinsed out the brushes for the last time and put them away in the cupboard under the stairs. We sat by our new gas fire in our milky white living room and had a glass of wine to celebrate. In the morning we would go into town and choose a carpet to replace threadbare 1960s broadloom. It was all done.

A few hours later, the bed juddered. The window rattled and the wooden frame around our lives creaked like a little boat on a choppy ocean. We were asleep, in that deep early morning dreaming. The window was open for the first time that spring, leaf budding on the sycamores that overhang the back fence, a blackbird singing — though that has no significance: there is a blackbird that sings most nights, persuaded by the city lights that it lives in one continuous brilliant day. The window rattled and we stirred. The creaking accelerated and with it a deep booming rose through the floor, through bed and pillow, felt in the bone, rather than heard, as the building jolted.

'Earthquake!' we yelled over the din, stumbling from dreaming to the doorway which, we had learned in childhood, was the safest place. The floor bucked beneath bare feet. It rolled up and down and sideways simultaneously as we fought for balance, and all around was the deafening confusion of things smashing and crashing and threatening to fall: weatherboard, roofing tiles, brick chimney. We clung to the doorframe and to one another. And then the quake dwindled to a stop and the building settled to a gentle swaying.

'Whooo . . .' we said. 'That was a big one.' Perhaps The Big One, the one we had been expecting all our lives. The quake that would hit us somewhere, sometime in this fault-crazed country. Every time the earth jolted, we thought it had arrived at our rattling door. The Big One. That instant when somewhere beneath our feet one massive tectonic plate shifted in its grinding fashion, and rock buckled, chasms opened, and tiny particles of sandstone separated and flowed to the surface like water. Ever since the nature study projects when we traced EARTHQUAKE in Letraset capitals and coloured them in with our Lakeland pencils. We drew little pictures of houses falling over and tiny people running to accompany the facts copied from the blackboard: Wellington, 8.2, 1855. Murchison, 7.8, 1929. Napier, 7.8, 1931. We knew about the land rising round Wellington Harbour, making room for a road and a railway, and how the basin where ships anchored had drained and been turned into a cricket pitch — which meant that on the whole that earthquake had been a good thing, though someone did get squashed flat by a chimney. We knew about the dust and fires in Napier, and how an old man had been lifted from the rubble after being buried for three days, and about the poor animals in Murchison who had been buried by slips and floods. We knew we lived on a precarious crust no more substantial than the meringue of a pavlova. We did volcanoes too, with drawings of the Pink and White Terraces, and a model of Ruapehu in papier-mâché with a torch in the middle shining through red cellophane for molten earth.

We contemplated the stern black-and-white images in our *School Journal*s that showed our country as a giant fish drawn up by a muscled god with his legs braced against the thwarts of a tippy-looking canoe, and knew that this was true in its way: as true as alpine faults and magma. We lived on a shuddery inconstant place where ordinary people could be travelling home at Christmas with all their presents wrapped in shiny paper on the luggage rack, and the train might plunge without warning into a hole in a bridge because a volcano upstream has released a sudden flood. We had seen the pictures in the *Weekly News*: all the second-class passengers had been washed away, and all their presents. We had been well taught not to place our faith in solid ground.

We had also been taught more pragmatically how to keep safe in this precarious world. When we felt the first shudderings we were to hide under our desks or stand in a doorway. We have since been told that this is not necessarily a good idea: it may be preferable simply to roll from your bed and lie on the floor by its big comfortable bulk, within the triangle of safety, like a lamb in a storm beside its big mother. And as close as possible to an exterior wall so that you too may be that person who is lifted from the ruins covered in white dust but unharmed after days of entombment. But the habit is ingrained: when the quake struck that spring night, we clung to the doorway. It did not snap, the tiles did not rain down, and when the shaking ceased we went downstairs and the staircase was still attached to the wall.

The kitchen floor glittered with broken glass as if it had been struck by a heavy, unseasonable frost, and every wall was covered in a deep web of cracks exposing plaster the exact tint of old grey knickers. But our books were safe, piled under a drop cloth, and the row of little swans from the mantelpiece and the windows had stayed unbroken. The bare lightbulb swung gently to and fro, the light washing up one wall then over another of broken milky white.

We went out onto the street where our neighbours stood about touseled and confused in their pyjamas. The young couple who had just moved in on one side, the old friends in the adjoining flat. The street was lit for some way, then slammed abruptly into blackout. Stars shone bright and metallic in an inky sky. The air was shrill with alarms — car alarms, house alarms — and somewhere in the dark the sirens started.

What do you do at such a time? Well, first, you make a cup of tea. Who knows how long the power will stay on in your area? You fill the kettle and switch it on. You switch on the radio which is still talking happily to itself up in Wellington, spinning

Classic Hits: with fine but unintentional irony — The Beach Boys. 'Good Vibrations.' Eventually it wakes up and begins to broadcast texts from Christchurch which are all really the same message: of things falling, children crying, cars driving in the dark to find higher ground. Eventually the television too stirs into life with bleary pre-dawn footage of rubble, a flashlit shot of a broken church, and — isn't that the bagel shop round the corner? And the fish and chip shop? Both shorn of their Edwardian frontages which have fallen down flat onto the street, leaving their interiors exposed to public gaze like a couple of dolls' houses? The numbers begin: a 7.4, later revised to 7.1, its epicentre thirty kilometres west of the city, a previously unsuspected fault buried beneath deposits of shingle, inactive for at least 16,000 years.

So we had been wrong in our first assumption: this was not after all The Big One, but a lesser cousin. This fault line is a mere twenty-five kilometres long, and the size of a quake is in direct proportion to the length of its fault. The longer the fault, the larger the quake. The Alpine Fault is 400 kilometres long. When it shifts, the quake will be at least ten times bigger than our little shake. It will be an 8. An 8-plus. So The Big One still waits in the wings, like some heavy villain twirling his moustache.

So, what do you do now?

While the images rotate and the text messages repeat, you get dressed. You sweep up broken glass. The sun comes up. You ring family who live in other places and might see the news and worry. We're fine, we're fine. You ring friends. The friend whose husband was consumed by despair over the past winter and jumped from a cliff: how is she, in their house overlooking the ocean? Fine, she says. I'm fine. And a friend whose husband had a stroke five years ago. The kitchen cupboards have fallen away from the walls, the windows are smashed; she stood in her bedroom doorway in the dark for two hours till the sun rose, while her husband walked about the house saying over and over, 'Broken, broken.' I'm fine, she says. You ring friends who moved a few years ago from Geneva to a remote bay on the Peninsula. We're fine, they say. Nothing broken except a bust of Voltaire that slid from a shelf and smashed to the floor. Down the telephone the voices of friends are almost unrecognisable: high-pitched with relief, like the voices of breathless children.

What else can you do?

You put all the books back on the shelves.

It's a familiar reflex. When my mother died, for instance, I tidied her house. I wiped benches, I dusted shelves and folded all her clothes, and stacked her pots and pans in the cupboards. She had always been a woman who kept things: our old school uniforms lay neatly folded in a cupboard, as if we might suddenly revert from being middle-aged women with jobs and families of our own to teenagers moodily picking at pimples and listening to the transistor. The transistor was there too, in a cardboard box, along with a bundle of the aerogrammes we sent at infrequent intervals once we flew away from her, and her nurse's heavy serge cape with its scarlet lining, and a textbook with alarming photos of tonsils blackened by diphtheria and children polka dotted with measles. I dumped the transistor in the bin. It never went properly, even back in 1965. I emptied the laundry shelves of old bottles of stove polish and pots of congealed paint. 'Stop it!' my sister yelled at me. 'Just stop it!' She wanted to be quiet and think about the funeral, but I couldn't stop. I was Mickey's mop, fetching and emptying on busy stumpy legs. It felt necessary to straighten what could be straightened now that our mother had died, her breath rattling in. Pause. And out.

The quake, while powerful, did not possess the seismic force of that tiny rattling breath, but it had been unnerving nevertheless. There was a bright metallic sheen to the day, a kind of sequined artificiality. This day could fly apart in an instant. I needed to put all the books back in order, fiction on the right, non-fiction arranged by subject, poetry on the left. I threw out all the books I had kept merely from habit or because they had been a gift. Into the bin went the books by the author who had behaved scurrilously to another writer. Into the bin went the badly written poems, the boring travelogues, the novels putrid with misogyny. Then we moved the furniture back from the middle of the room where it had stood while we painted, and opened the door to let in the brittle day. Roof tiles and chimney bricks covered the garden, and the damp earth trembled with the first of thousands of aftershocks. (There were ninety-eight that day alone.) Though perhaps it was not the earth but your own body that was shaking. I filled a glass with water and placed it on the windowsill: if the water shimmered or splashed I could tell the difference. It seemed important to be able to distinguish between perceived and actual sensation.

The radio and television were broadcasting reports of sewage leaking into living rooms, houses rendered unlivable, people without power or water, silt volcanoes exploding in fields and city streets, roads split by gaping crevices in which children posed for the television. A man stopped outside our own kitchen and took a photograph of our broken chimney. Another was carefully framing a shot of a crack in the footpath across the road.

We needed to go out and see for ourselves. It wasn't *schadenfreude*, some creepy desire to cheer ourselves up by witnessing other people's greater disaster. It felt instead as if we were small animals who had been frightened in a great storm. We needed to emerge from our burrow and see what remained of our little world.

We went out for a walk.

-----〰〰〰-----

FLOWERS

The room is white and
every wall is flowering.
White flowers frame
each window. White
flowers pour from

cracks in the ceiling.
Flowers grow, sleek
and silken as water
lilies in the dark
beneath the bed.
Their seed drifts
like thistledown.
Soft multitudes
float, catch in the
throat. Their seeds
tickle your damp
crevices, looking
for a place to grow.
They put out a
skinny toe.
White.
It reaches
all the
way
down.

Blossom hung over fallen walls, pink camellias lined the driveways of Edwardian villas with gashes in their roofs where the chimneys had fallen through. The river flowed high and fast and milky white between banks of daffodils and budding willow. A woman was walking quickly along the path by the park. She was going home, she said, to check on her Lange pots. She liked those pots. And then she told us about being in Spain for the Olympics and how someone came into the room she was sharing with three other girls and stole their handbags — all except hers, because she was sleeping on a top bunk and had her bag tightly clasped against her chest. She'd been wearing pink babydoll pyjamas that her mother had sewn for her trip: pink, with broderie anglaise trim . . . She walked off rapidly along the path by the river to check on her pots.

Plastic ribbon cordoned off sections of Victoria Street. People wandered and paused to talk. It could almost have been a party. They gathered in front of Caxton Press with its broken balustrade and the bagel shop which had indeed lost its frontage. They raised cameras and took digital shots of naked rooms, a touseled bed. They viewed the wreckage of the hairdresser's and the church with its fallen cross.

The coffee shop on the corner by the clock tower was serving coffee in paper cups until the water was reconnected. We sat in the sun and talked to a young friend, an artist, tall and Dutch, whose work is tall too and requires big walls. His flat — a big old mercantile building — lay across the road. Literally. We could see it from our table: a pile of bricks and rubble. He had escaped certain death by deciding to spend the night at his girlfriend's place. We laughed with relief at his escape. Thank god, we said. Thank god! We laughed with relief at our own escape. Buildings had fallen or been damaged, but no one had been killed. Thank god, we said, thank god for the escape of the entire city.

It was so sturdy, set down with that breathtaking nineteenth-century confidence on a stretch of primeval swamp in a regular grid about a central square. The founding fathers stood about at the intersections, cast in bronze and looking suitably sombre, though in reality they had been lads in their twenties, playing at the kind of games now reserved for the gaming console. Create Your Own City! Build an Empire! Only they had played with real people and real buildings of stone and mortar. The cathedral was Victorian Gothic, with a skinny spire. The university had quadrangles, like the ones its founders had so recently left behind, of heavy grey basalt carved from the hills on the city's eastern flank where a couple of volcanoes leaned companionably back to back, offering an indented coastline for sheltered anchorage and hills covered in eminently millable timber.

The city grew into its grid, the wealthy in leafy suburbs to the west, poorer folk to the south and east where flax and toetoe were replaced by tarmac and rows of low weatherboard homes. On the coast, seaside settlements sprang up among the sand dunes and along the cliff tops. The city had a reputation for being steady, rather stuffy, subject to petty yet deeply felt provincial snobberies.

What Christchurch did not have was a reputation for being earthquake prone. That was the prerogative of Wellington, where most of the downtown area stands on land that lay below the ocean until the quake of 1855. Napier too had had its quake, and Auckland has its dormant volcanoes. But Christchurch was unlikely to startle anyone.

Then a small fault moved one morning, leaving a jagged tear across the flat green paddocks out at Greendale, and here we were: chimneys fallen, cracks in the walls, and dense white stinking silt bubbling up through fractured tarmac and carefully tended lawns, or bursting into the air like geysers from nibbled pasture.

But no one had died. Thank god, we said.

Though that was just a reflex. Just an expression of relief. We were not really thanking a beneficent deity for our young artist friend's survival, any more than we believed a divine creator had unleashed the quake for his mysterious purpose in the first place. The cause of the quake was tectonic, the absence of death down to sheer luck. God had nothing to do with it, though over the next week there were letters to the paper suggesting that he had had a specific interest in targeting the brothels of Manchester Street, and the comment column on Yahoo! filled with prayers and god bless. At Sunday services across the city, thanks were given to the Divine Engineer who had inspired the designers of the earthquake-proofing that kept most of the city's buildings intact. In Haiti, an earthquake of the same force had demolished 280,000 buildings and killed a quarter of a million people. In Kobe, a 6.8 in 1995 had demolished 200,000 buildings, killed 6500 people and wrecked a major port. Thank god for building codes and reinforced concrete! Thank god!

But for most of us, in this age, in this place, it was just an expression.

It was not always so.

When I have been upset, I tidy, I walk. And I look things up.
I try to understand. I try to fit words around feeling, take notes,
make poems, write things down. As we were walking back to our
damaged flat that morning, something was tugging at my mind.

Voltaire.

That plaster bust of the philosopher with his long comical nose
and his hooded eyes. The bust that had slipped from our friends'
house at Decanter Bay and smashed to bits. Wasn't he caught up
somehow in an earthquake? The Lisbon earthquake? A vague
memory from long-distant French classes. *Candide* ... The book
was on the shelf in the newly arranged fiction section along with
some other old textbooks: a copy of *Twelfth Night*, Johnson's
Rasselas, *Sweet's Anglo-Saxon Primer*. Books I had kept for some
reason but not opened since 1968. The margins of *Candide* were
scribbled with notes in a neater, younger hand than my current
scrawl. My name was in the front: Fiona Farrell. 95 York Place,
Dunedin. And in the preface there it was: a long poem, *sur le
désastre de Lisbonne*, accompanied by a steel engraving of tiny
boats tossed on huge waves, tiny people raising their arms from
the water for rescue, and a city skyline burning in curling heraldic
flames.

The first of November 1755. Now, that was a Big One.
An 8-plus, a 9. The Lisbon earthquake sent cracks not just
through the masonry of a city but through the entire edifice of
European thought. And God was most definitely at its centre.

There is an eyewitness account of the event written by an English clergyman, Charles Davy, who was on a visit to the city. It was All Saints' Day. A beautiful day. 'The sun shone out in its full lustre: the whole face of the sky was perfectly serene and clear.'

Davy was 'between the hours of nine and ten set down in my apartment, just finishing a letter, when the papers and the table I was writing on began to tremble with a gentle motion, which rather surprised me as I could not perceive a breath of wind stirring'. The house then began to shake 'from the very foundation', which he at first presumed to be the vibration of coaches passing on the road outside, then recognised as an earthquake on account of the 'strange frightful kind of noise underground'. He had heard that sound before during a quake in Madeira. He stood, not sure whether to run outside or stay in, since both he knew could be risky. But the decision was made for him: there came a 'most horrid crash as if every edifice in the city had tumbled down at once'. His own house shook so violently that the upper storeys collapsed, and through the falling stone he saw the sky disappear into an 'Egyptian darkness' caused by the dust raised by the 'violent concussion'. Davy struggled through the narrow ruined streets to the banks of the Tagus where, like many other citizens, he hoped to find greater safety in the open. There he found 'all ranks and conditions . . . ladies half dressed and some without shoes', priests who had run from the altars in their sacerdotal vestments, for the city had been at mass when the quake struck. Fearful citizens knelt by the river, striking their breasts and crying *'misericórdia meu Deus!'* A second violent shock caused greater panic, and this was followed forty minutes later by 'a large body of water, rising as it were like a mountain'. It rolled into the estuary, gathering up ships at anchor, and sweeping away all those people who had taken refuge on boats on the harbour and around the newly constructed quays. 'They were all swallowed up as in a whirlpool and never more appeared.' Two further waves added to the devastation.

Davy headed back into the city, where cracks and fissures had opened, some releasing 'like a jet stream a large quantity of fine white sand to a prodigious height'. One crack was so wide that three streets of houses disappeared into it before another shock drew the earth back over. He made his way to the Mint which 'being a low and very strong building' had received little damage. There he discovered a young man about seventeen years of age, still standing guard, keeping safe the millions of money within. Fires had broken out across the city, lit, some suspected, by 'a gang of hardened villains who had been confined and got out of prison when the wall fell at the first shock', though Davy — as a good Protestant — was more convinced that the cause lay on the altars lit with hundreds of candles for the mass of All Saints' Day. Cooking fires also contributed. 'The whole number of persons that perished including those who were burnt or afterwards crushed to death while digging in the ruins is supposed on the lowest calculation to amount to more than sixty thousand.' The 'vast and opulent city' of Lisbon had been reduced to ruins.

I cannot read this account or look at Le Bas's engraving of the city engulfed by waves and fire without feeling sick. I feel as queasy as when I look at that jumpy black-and-white film of the 1964 Alaska quake on YouTube. A sailor on a ship in the harbour is filming some kids mucking about on the wharf. There are a couple of dogs. A sailor is throwing them lollies. The camera jolts as the quake — a hundred times stronger than the quake that toppled the bagel shop — strikes the city. The camera turns to record the harbour emptying of water, a ship sinking to the gunnels in a crack, a wavery line on the horizon that builds rapidly until the wave washes over everything, and still he is recording in that grim, funereal black and white.

No wonder, I think, reading Davy's account and looking at Le Bas's engraving, that the King of Portugal, Joseph I, simply refused to enter a building ever again. He moved his entire court to tents on a hillside near the city and there they remained till his death over twenty years later in 1777. The Lisbon quake, centred beneath the Atlantic, 200 kilometres off Cap Saint Vincent, was felt throughout Europe as far as Finland. New ways of building cities emerged as a response, including the use of the 'Pomballian box', named for the man responsible for the rebuilding of Lisbon, the Marquis de Pombal. Working fast, using the expertise of military engineers, haphazard medieval structures were replaced with a rational simplicity: streets were straight and wide. The unstable ground most affected in the centre of the city was filled with a forest of wooden poles which, being constantly exposed to the seepage of salt water below ground, remained pliant and resistant to rot. And on this reinforced land new buildings rose, each built about a cube of vertical, horizontal and diagonal bracing, like a cube of interlocking Union Jacks. The buildings were prefabricated outside the city, then transported to site. Their design was uniform: four storeys high, an arcade at ground level with shops, apartments above with balconies, and between each building there was a fire-resistant wall. No ornament — an edict that infuriated the wealthier citizens wedded to ostentation. The priorities were unequivocal. Lisbon's citizens were to be housed thenceforth in buildings that were rational: well lit and ventilated, and above all safe. The design was tested by soldiers who marched about the prototype in unison to simulate the shaking of a quake. In their new homes, the citizens of an enlightened city could sleep easy amidst beauty and coherence. The quake had shaken down old edifices and replaced them with a social and philosophical ideal expressed in wood and stone. New ways of thinking emerged from the cracks and fissures in old belief.

Why did God permit this catastrophe to happen?

It was three weeks before Voltaire in distant France learned of the event. The news travelled toward him slowly, at the speed of a horse or a human walking: four miles an hour, maybe seven at speed. When he learned of the destruction and loss of life, the philosopher set to work on a lengthy poetic treatise, in rhyming couplets, in which he attacked the proposition of the German philosopher Leibniz that we live in a benign and orderly universe under the governance of a kindly disposed deity.

'All is for the best,' Leibniz had proposed. He called this stance 'optimism', inventing the word. Like other 'isms' — communism, socialism — 'optimism' was an intellectual mechanism for interpreting what happens to us. (Its opposite, 'pessimism', was a later invention, its first citation in English usually given as a letter from Coleridge to Southey.)

Voltaire opens his attack on this 'optimism' with a cannonade of exclamations, attacking

> *Philosophes trompés qui crient: 'Tout est bien!'*
> Deluded philosophers who cry: 'All is well!'

Just look, he says, at the ruined city, the women and children under broken marble. How can you say that this is the work of a just God? If this is a punishment for vice, what sin has the baby at its mother's breast committed? And was Lisbon any more sinful than London or Paris? Yet Lisbon has been

> *. . . abîmée, et l'on danse à Paris.*
> . . . plunged into the abyss, while they dance in Paris.

Over the following 230 lines, the philosopher builds his argument, struggling with the notion of divine design. The death of a man may in the general scheme have a beneficent purpose, nourishing a thousand insects, but does this knowledge offer any true consolation? No: the world is chaos, and the truth is that we are

> *Un faible composé de nerfs et d'ossements*
> *Ne peut être insensible au choc des éléments:*
> *Ce mélange de sang, de liqueurs et de poudre,*
> *Puisqu'il fut assemblé, fut fait pour se dissoudre.*
> A feeble being composed of nerves and bone,
> Unable to withstand elemental shock:
> This blend of blood, fluids and powder,
> That is assembled, only to dissolve.

The thinking leads him to that fundamental question:

> *Que suis-je? où vais-je, et d'où suis-je tiré?*
> What am I? where am I going, and from whence did
> I come?

Though the French is more visual, *tirer* suggesting being drawn forth, as a baby is drawn from its mother. There is a hint of a slippery little body being assisted into the light.

Voltaire proposes an unadorned answer: we are simply

> *Atomes tourmentés sur cet amas de boue,*
> *Que la mort engloutit et dont le sort se joue.*
> Tormented atoms on a pile of mud,
> Whom death will swallow up and whom fate plays with
> at will.

But in our very frailty and vulnerability, there is nobility. We are atoms, yes, but we are thinking atoms —

> ... *atomes pensants, atomes dont les yeux,*
> *Guidés par la pensée, ont mesuré les cieux.*
> ... thinking atoms, whose eyes,
> Guided by the capacity for thought, have measured the
> heavens.

The argument at this point seems to be heading toward a godless universe but at the last moment veers away from that conclusion. Voltaire was a man of the eighteenth century after all and perhaps it was too soon for complete godlessness. He ends instead with what looks to me like equivocation: we may be deluded in believing that all is for the best, but we retain one thing that makes life tolerable: hope. Once he could have been less sanguine, but now he is old and — *autres temps, autres moeurs* — he needs to believe that, if not now, at some time in the future all will indeed be well.

It feels like a bit of an anti-climax after the blood, fluids and soluble powder — though even this equivocal conclusion proved too much for Rousseau, who published a rebuttal in 1756, objecting to Voltaire's despair and insisting that it was human error that caused the devastation in Lisbon. It was human designers who had assembled 20,000 houses of six or seven storeys in that confined place. Had the inhabitants been housed less densely, the losses would have been fewer: they could have fled inland, and next morning they would have been discovered alive and as cheerful as ever. Besides, Rousseau adds, is sudden death the very worst that can happen to a human being? Perhaps people who died at Lisbon were spared a more painful and lingering demise later on?

Rousseau insists on a beneficent deity, an afterlife, a world where individual pain is subsumed to the greater good, where a human dies, and in death nourishes the growth of plants and animals and ultimately other humans. This is nature's order and we are part of it.

> *Je la sens, je la crois, je la veux, je l'espère, je la défenderai jusqu'a mon dernier soupir . . .*

I feel it, I believe it, I wish for it, I hope for it, I will defend it to my last breath . . .

I sat in our flat with its cracked walls, waiting for a builder friend of our neighbours' to come and fix a tarpaulin over the gap in the roof where the chimney fell in. At midday we had driven over to Mitre 10 where they were doing a fine trade in tarpaulins and sheets of plywood. We had borrowed a ladder from next door and tried to fit the plastic ourselves, but it felt a very long way from the ground. We were too timid to do it properly, and strong winds were predicted. So we waited for Hayden and I read a couple of eighteenth-century philosophers arguing about an earthquake in elegant aphorisms. Like two men duelling to the death, feint and parry, according to strict rules of deportment. I stacked the chimney bricks that had flown from the roof in a pile by the back door. Silt covered the back lawn, a fine grey mud smelling like buried river stone. I piled the bricks and thought: an atom on a pile of mud.

PANEGYRIC

He's the Minister of Earthquakes
and Tectonic Upheaval.
His portfolio is Forces
Chthonic and Primeval.

The pilot of our sinking ship,
the shepherd of our flock.
The man to lead us safe
between hard place and
fallen rock. He's the man
who wears the hard hat.
The man who has the plan.
The man who hands out
contracts. The man who
says who can. The man
who cannot be opposed.
The man who knows what
no one knows: who sees
which way the earth tilts,
and how the hard winds blow.
The Minister of all that falls,
of blood and broken bone,
of tidal wave and tumbled wall,
silt and shattered stone.
A prophet for his people,
he'll have his statue in the Square,
beside the fallen steeple,
beneath the broken stair.
The hills bow down,
the oceans kneel
before his mighty rod.
Panjandrum. Plenipotentate.
And next in line to God.

Five months after that first quake, another fault line ruptured.

I was driving south. I had been in the city to discuss a book. There had been one published soon after the September quake, but it was all fallen buildings and photographs of men in hard hats and high-viz vests. I was going to write the text for a different kind of book, a photographic book with portraits of ordinary people and their stories of the quake. People like young friends who had lain in their bed in the dark out at Brighton, cuddling their little son and telling him stories as they waited for whatever might come: morning light, or a tsunami rolling in from Pegasus Bay over the sand dunes. And the elderly friend who had run out into the dark but decided, standing there in her faded pyjamas under the clothesline, that this was not the way she wanted to die. She is a woman of spirit, one who had stood in the centre of a rugby pitch back in 1981 in a tight knot of protestors as several thousand Waikato fans bayed for blood. Death in pallid Viyella was not for her. So she had gone back into her home, fumbled about for her best angora sweater — the one everyone says makes her eyes look very, very blue — and her best trousers. She had applied a hopeful slash of crimson lipstick. And then she had lain down beneath the duvet, properly prepared. Then there was the story of the friend of someone we met at a party who had come home late, slept right through the quake and woken to find her flat wrecked: that morning she had rung the police to report an exceedingly messy burglary.

Those were the kinds of stories for this book. It was the right time to tell them. The quake was safely distant. There had been aftershocks, dozens, then hundreds, then thousands until we had stopped counting. They rattled down the valley, slammed into the house, shook it about, then carried on out into the wide Pacific. That's a 4.2, we'd say. A 3.8. If they hit when we were in bed, we no longer bothered to run for the doorway. We heard the vibration through the pillow, stirred and went back to sleep.

The city had taken on a superficial normality.

Children went back to school, the littlest clutching their teddies. The mayor was returned in that year's local body elections with a majority vastly increased by nightly appearances on primetime television clad in flak jacket and hard hat, fluently bidding everyone to pull together. National politicians flew down for a never-to-be-repeated photo opportunity, looking serious and purposeful among the rubble, ideally in the company of a passing All Black. Businesses reopened, though some had to relocate to obscure parts of the city. Rentals for those premises in the inner city that had remained intact increased, sometimes astronomically. Our favourite bookshop, confronted with an increase it could not afford, moved to a space next to a video arcade and Cineplex, the books in piles at cut price and the air thick and sticky with popcorn. Other shops went out of business altogether. You went to buy something — cheese, a t-shirt, the warrant for the car — only to find the place barricaded by scaffolding, or broken and empty, its windows bandaged with crisscrossed sticky tape. But no one was camping on the streets as they were in Haiti. Cholera and typhoid had not taken hold. The general outlines of the city remained intact. It was like one of those television makeovers, extreme but recoverable: you had simply to wait for the bandages to be removed and new fresh skin to be revealed.

And day after day the earth rearranged itself, the aftershocks rippling and recorded on Geonet, each one like a bubble bursting to the surface of a spring. We learned how to consult the geographical co-ordinates to find the exact location of each quake, the exact house address beneath whose garden the earth had shifted. The experts reassured us that a host of tiny releases was desirable to prevent the tension beneath the earth building to intolerable levels. So we indulged them as they roared down the valley, said BOO!, then headed for the open ocean. There was even a kind of exhilaration. It was simply so powerful, this force that roared out from a break in the earth's crust to lift us up, 150 kilometres distant, on the other side of the remains of a massive volcano. Power that had not been released for at least, the experts told us, 16,000 years. And we had been on the earth to experience it. How amazing!

At a more practical level, there were reports in the press of delays in insurance assessments and inequalities in the attentions of bureaucrats. In the eastern suburbs, built on swamp where the liquefaction had been extreme, streets remained coated in silt and houses slumped at awkward angles. Friends described family members living in lopsided kitchens, or crammed together in garages, caravans or one or two livable rooms. People remained without water, without toilets. Portaloos were placed at intervals along the verges, but there were complaints that there were not nearly enough. Buckets were distributed with plastic bags for disposal in bins at the end of the street. Complaints began to gather around the commission charged with assessing damage for insurance purposes. Many of the inspectors had been recruited from Australia, including a large number of ex-detectives employed at over $80 an hour by a Queensland company called Verifact which specialises in investigating claims for workplace accident insurance. Their primary objective is to detect fraud, their fundamental stance doubt. There was talk of qualified local people — builders, architects, engineers — being turned down in favour of Australian mates. There were complaints of contradictory advice, vagueness, indecision . . .

After the sharp shock of the quake itself, we had moved onto the messy and long-drawn-out process of reconstruction. The quake was past. We could attend to commemoration.

That day, I drove south, heading to Dunedin where I had a literary residency for a year, feeling pleased that the editorial meeting had gone well. I would work on the earthquake book, collecting the stories of ordinary people and their extraordinary courage. I sat in the car, thinking about it, planning how it would go. Just out of the city, at Dunsandel, I stopped for lunch. Coffee and a pork pie.

That was when a second fault line ruptured — also short, some kilometres distant from the first, but shallow and abrupt. The café at Dunsandel is an old general store, built of weatherboard a hundred years ago. It flexed mightily. Bottles of wine and apple juice rattled on their shelves. The woman behind the till moved toward the door. I stood, poised for flight. But everyone else in the store remained exactly where they were. The man in the corner turned the page of his magazine; the group at the back table paused, laughed — then continued talking.

'Locals!' said a woman next to me who was from Auckland. And I felt a ridiculous little flicker of pleasure. We were so unflappable, so *southern*. I finished my pie. It was only when I was back in the car driving south and flicked on the radio that I realised our jolt at Dunsandel had caused carnage in the central city. Whole streets had crashed to the ground; the cathedral had collapsed, people were lying dead on Cashel Mall, were trapped beneath slabs of concrete in the CBD. I did a U-turn and headed for home — where my husband was safe after all: he had not gone into the city, as he had planned, to stock up at the supermarket with its canyons of bottles and cans, its avalanche of glass and steel. He had instead been standing on the main street in Akaroa where he had watched the quake roll toward him like the wash from a mighty ferry, tossing all the little wooden buildings on either side up into the air, then down again. But they survived with minor damage. He survived, and all our friends too, but there were other stories . . .

A young woman had died with her baby in her arms. A friend's son had dragged another young man from the rubble and lifted him on a makeshift stretcher made from a door onto the roof of a police car, supporting him as they edged through dense traffic toward the hospital, but too late, too late . . . Friends had walked for hours — five hours, nine hours — across the city to find sons, daughters, wives, grandchildren, boyfriends. They had kicked off their shoes and walked barefoot through rubble and broken glass, part of that crowd of thousands all walking with fixed intent — everyone remembers the stare, the grey dust on face and hair and clothing, the silent determined walking — for that is what we do when a city falls and we are unharmed but operating purely on instinct, on pure impulse: we set off walking with fixed intent to find the people we love. Or we cycle on borrowed bikes along broken streets, where gaping holes have opened in the tarmac into which cars have nosedived like dead beasts in a waterhole. People walked back to homes where boulders had rolled down from the hilltops and crushed the living room, where roofs had collapsed or cracks had opened. Everyone walking along roads that had buckled to the contours of old river beds to find children, a wife, a husband, to get back home.

Death was so very close. People had been crushed beneath concrete slabs or masonry or those rocks that rolled from the steep volcanic hills. Students at a city language school had sent texts of unbearable poignancy from beneath a great shifting mound of concrete to their families in Japan, China, the Philippines, and then gone silent. A friend at the *Press* described on radio finding his way from a collapsing building and walking across the city to find his wife: there was a man, he said, lying beneath a fallen verandah. He had noticed the dead man's shoes. How brightly polished they were.

A cordon was flung about the city. And there it remains as I write this, weeks later. The buildings lie in ruins, and with them all the invisible routines that humans create around buildings: the walk across the Square to visit friends, to go a movie. The cafés, the shop with the lovely shoes, the optician's, the library. Businesses lie inaccessible beyond wire gates and ribbons of orange plastic manned by Army and Air Force personnel with military vehicles, trucks and tanks. High-rise buildings tilt and threaten to tumble. Our flat, like thousands of others, is set for demolition, its walls fallen in, its floor buckled on unsteady ground. Whole suburbs are slumping into the swampy earth and the talk is no longer of reconstruction, but of relocation. Reconstruction might be a sensible response to the destruction wrought by war, for example. A war has a beginning and it has an end, totally determined by human will. Earthquakes observe another schedule entirely. Once a fault has shifted, others are placed under strain, and there are so very many lying under our feet. A map of Canterbury's fault lines resembles a porcelain plate covered with a web of crazing. The city has been built upon a swamp and could continue to startle us. Relocation may be the only option the earth leaves us.

But that, like any other decision, is fraught with difficulty. This quake, like Lisbon's, has a social context. Geologically, it is unremarkable. This country is as jumpy as a canoe on a restless ocean, as unpredictable as a great fish that could sound at any moment and carry us all with it into chaos. Once, creatures who found themselves clinging to its surface as the earth cracked and boulders tumbled down from the tops would simply have taken themselves off to some other place drier and less alarming. But we inhabit a less flexible universe, governed by particular social mechanisms.

In Lisbon, a marquis and a few army engineers redesigned a city, and within a year it was taking its new shape. But in 2011 the pace and quality of reconstruction in a small Western democracy is dictated not by government but by company profits. A minister has been appointed to oversee the city's recovery and given powers of veto and direction unprecedented in peacetime, but as a man committed to a contemporary philosophy of economic supremacy, he concedes without demurral to the marketplace: what happens in the city, he says, is all 'over to the insurers'. So the city's future is taking shape in boardrooms in Brisbane or New York, while all around you hear the bright voices of people cracking under strain, people living in broken houses, people losing jobs as firms go out of business, children disturbed and unable to sleep. A friend tells you about the giant fungi that her daughter found growing along the skirting boards beneath her children's beds in Halswell: great floppy shiny blooms in the dark. 'It can't be good for the kids,' she says. 'Breathing in that stuff.'

There is no exhilaration in this.

Atoms on mud.

Maybe I haven't understood Voltaire properly. My French is shaky and I am definitely not a philosopher. Here I am in a little valley on a peninsula, with hens pecking about at the door and the sound of the sea at my back. I cut up pumpkin for tea as the bench shimmies a little (a 3.2, maybe a 3.3 . . .) and I am thinking as I slice through the tough orange rind about Voltaire and earthquakes, houses falling into holes in the ground, women with no shoes running through a fallen city, and about the jolt that out here at Otanerito split the house in two, leaving a neat five-centimetre crack round the whole circumference of walls and ceiling, smashed all our china, ripped the water tank from the roof, and tipped my preserves in a sweet sludge across the floor, purple and gold like a spreading bruise. I find the black casserole and butter it, crush some garlic. What do I feel? Here, as I am chopping up a pumpkin and the bench shimmies? Or when I am in the city, walking along its broken streets?

I feel small. Shaken. I feel as if I am no longer standing on solid ground. I am not earthed, nor balanced — all those words we use to describe a desirable human state. I am, instead, rattled. Unsteady. Unstable.

But along with this destabilising has come an intense sensation of being intricately linked to others. To strangers like the woman with her Lange pots and the people whose bright voices crack as they talk of making the best of things, clinging to optimism as to a faith. To friends like the young man who might have been crushed had he not chosen to spend the night in his girlfriend's warm bed, and the friends who helped us shovel silt from our flat, wearing borrowed clothes because their own clothes hang in an apartment they have not been able to enter for two months. The feeling extends to people I have never met: to people in Baghdad, bombed into desolation, and people who went through the Blitz and people who came home from the trenches and people who came home from Alamein and people flooded in New Orleans or Queensland and the tiny people racing in tiny cars just ahead of that surging silent littered wave in Japan, the people whose lives have been tumbled sideways by mudslide or eruption.

An earthquake is a natural event. The feeling is not contaminated by anger: no one decided over a couple of after-dinner whiskies to inflict shock and awe on this city. No one signed a contract on its destruction. The feeling is simply of insignificance before nature, of being part of a vast and constantly evolving system so complex it might as well be chaos. Except that I choose to keep imposing upon it my own tiny patterns.

When I was a child, I lay in bed looking for the faces that lurked in the paisley frieze that ran around my bedroom wall. In that drifting state between sleep and waking it was possible to make out strange creatures with paws and wings and, in the patch where the pattern joined just above the dressing table, a face with a bulbous nose and curly hair. Your eyes could play the same trick with the random streaks in the linoleum on the kitchen floor and in the knots in the boards on the back of the lavatory door. That's what I do now when faced with the randomness of ordinary life: I insist that unrelated details arrange themselves into something I am capable of recognising. I collect detail, assemble figures, read books and newspaper reports, talk to people, find patterns to which I can give a name. I try to write it down. Lines and circles forming in orderly rows across a blank white page.

So what does that leave for the atom moving about on a pile of mud?

Well, it leaves the present moment. Gold leaf, a pumpkin in a black casserole, the sound of the sea breathing in and out. In and out.

Just that.

THE SUITCASE

When we leave, we take the city
with us. Her bandaged buildings
and her gappy streets lurching
like some old gal who has been
knocked about. Her broken teeth,
black eye. Her shops with their
empty shelves. Her sewers and
their secret, soggy shambles.

We run away from her. Cross
over to the safe side where the
centre holds. Pretty cities
where marigolds will live
for ever. We breathe the scent
of white sheets in a quiet hotel.
But when the suitcase opens,

it's all there: bricks, the lost
dog, the old gal wheezing her
crazed song down a broken
alley. Something about dust
and ashes and how things
fall. We catch the whiff of
her among our folded socks.

Epilogue
May 2011

I was writing a book. A travel book. About walking. It took a year. Things happened.

When it was barely begun, the phone rang. Late February. 6 a.m. The sun was not yet up. The farmer in the next bay to the south was warning us that a tsunami was on its way. There had been a quake in Chile, which at such moments can feel almost neighbourly and close, like the far bank of a very large pond. A ripple was crossing the Pacific: in the narrow pocket bays of the Peninsula, hemmed by steep cliffs, it could build to great height. Once before when this happened — a South American earthquake, a succeeding tsunami — a cow shed had been lifted from its piles in Okains Bay and swept up the creek. It wasn't wise to take any chances.

So we raced about in the early morning dark, with two hours before the wave, keeping to its own mighty schedule, arrived on our shore. Waking guests, transporting them and their packs to higher ground, packing our car, deciding this and not that: computers, the memory stick with the text of my new book, our passports, bank cards, purse and wallet, all the photographs in the apple box where they had lingered for years awaiting that quiet winter day when they would all be stuck properly into albums. And some books, some clothes. And all my shoes. (I have narrow feet: it's difficult to find good shoes.) And my harp. And a thermos. And some toast. Briefly we considered the hens, but there are ten of them and there simply wasn't room: we propped the door to their coop open and left them to take their chances.

Then we drove up the road and waited at the corner where we could look down to our house sitting small and white as a hen on its nest by the unremarkable, ordinary sea. The sun shone. We sat on the grass beside the car and drank our tea and ate our toast. Birds sang among the trees down in the valley. The sheep moved placidly about the hillside. The hour of the wave approached. From our vantage point we watched as the water in the bay slowly withdrew, but no further than a low tide. The wet sand gleamed. After a while, it returned, unhurriedly. We could see it lapping at the little clay cliff that marks the edge between sand and paddock grass. No higher than a king tide. And that was it. We began to feel ridiculous sitting there with our thermos and the things that mattered stored in our car. A group of German backpackers in a rental car came round the corner. 'Nothing,' they said. They shrugged. They had their cameras. They were disappointed. Even we felt disappointed, though that was absurd. Did we really want our home to be swept from its piles? To be upturned into the creek? Our hens drowned, all our books flapping wet and unreadable along some unimaginable tide line? Yet still it felt oddly anti-climactic.

We came home again. We put the books and shoes and computers back in their places, and I went back to writing.

The travel book. About walking.

Over that winter, it assembled itself while things happened. My older daughter became pregnant with her first child and this time it stayed curled in her body and grew strongly: the size of a grain of rice, the size of a broad bean, the size of a tadpole with little hands and feet and big bulbous head, its tiny heart glittering like a moth's wing, beating fast. Across the world, my husband's mother shrank and died, and he went to England for her funeral. Friends fell in love, published books. One got married. One gave way to despair and jumped. The garden died to bare twigs. The rain fell and the road into the valley was rutted and muddy. I wrote at my desk as the willows outside the window blurred with green. Plum blossom covered the tree that never bears fruit. Lambs slid into the world on the damp green hillside.

And one night when we were staying at our flat in town, the earth shook and I found myself sweeping away broken glass, then reading a couple of eighteenth-century French philosophers arguing over the nature of God and humanity and the whole intricate mess of living as I waited for a builder to come and put a tarpaulin over the hole in our roof.

I read Rousseau's counter-argument. And I noticed him for the first time. He was a name, of course. One of those names I'd known for ages without having read him, like Dante. Some day I plan to read Dante. Some day I plan to read the *Odyssey*. And maybe more than the first two pages of Proust. I've read bits, I've seen movie adaptations of bits, I know more or less where they fit in the canon; I can perhaps quote a line or two. Madeleines: that's Proust. 'Man is born free but is everywhere in chains.' That's Rousseau. He was one of those writers who hovered like the people at a party whom you've seen about the place for years. Everyone else knows them. They have long familiar conversations. But you have never actually met. You've never sat opposite one another at a kitchen table among all the opened bottles and the remains of the quiche, and had a proper talk.

After the quake, I met Rousseau and, in particular, I met his last book.

Around twenty years after the Lisbon earthquake, and the philosophical thrust and parry with Voltaire over the nature of God that it engendered, Rousseau turned to something simpler. He began writing a sequence of reveries. *Les rêveries du promeneur solitaire* (*The Thoughts of the Solitary Walker*). He had been deeply unsettled by the criticism his work had received at the hands of clergy in both Paris and Geneva. His books had been burned in public. He had been driven into years of restless travel. But in the last two years of his life, in these final ten promenades, he writes calmly about the subject that has been central to his entire adult life: the nature of being human, and our relationship with the natural and spiritual worlds. The essays are of varying lengths, and written, he makes it quite clear, not primarily for an audience but for himself. He is simply trying to understand who he is when he is alone. The style of each piece catches the rhythm of a long walk, following a meandering thoughtful progress from one idea to another at a gentle pace. '*Me voici donc,* he begins, *seul sur la terre, n'ayant plus de frère, de prochain, d'ami, de société que moi-*

même' — 'So here I am alone on earth, having neither brother, nor companion, nor friend, nor any society except myself.'

He walks, finding in that quiet rhythmic movement in the open air, the ideal conditions for thought — like Mozart, who also found the ideal conditions for composition in solitary, rhythmic movement. In a letter to a friend, Mozart wrote that he composed most fluently when he was completely alone and 'truly himself': riding in a carriage, or walking after a good meal. That was when the musical ideas flowed most freely. Rousseau also found that walking animated and stimulated ideas. He could barely think, he said, when he was still. His body had to be moving in the open air for his mind to properly function. It was perhaps evidence of his Swiss origins, for in that country a little promenade on foot was regarded as fit recreation, whereas in France or England the gentry took their leisure on horseback. Walking amidst dramatic mountain scenery invigorated Rousseau. Botany absorbed him. It was while he was walking that he composed these essays, noting random thoughts as they occurred to him on the backs of playing cards he kept in his pocket for that purpose.

In the second promenade, Rousseau goes into greater detail about this process of thinking. He does not deliberately set out to create the conditions for thought: rather, they arise unexpectedly. For instance, one Thursday in October 1776 he had an accident while out walking in Paris. He does not describe it in any detail in the context of this promenade, but elsewhere the exact circumstances were recorded.

He had spent that afternoon walking through the hillside

vineyards on Ménilmontant (now the site of the enormous Père-Lachaise cemetery) looking for rare plants. Toward six in the evening, he was returning home when he was knocked to the ground by a Great Dane. It was the fashion then among the nobility to allow a large dog to run ahead of the carriage, presumably to scatter irritating pedestrians. The Great Dane preceded the carriage of the Baron de Saint-Fargeau, running, Rousseau's friend Corancez reported, with the speed of 'a rifle bullet'. Seeing it burst forth from an alarmed crowd, heading straight toward him, the philosopher's first impulse was to avoid collision by leaping over the dog's head. The dog, however, was too large and Rousseau was flung to the ground, knocking himself out on a cobblestone.

When he came to, he had no awareness of what had happened.

It was a moment of utter perfection.

He lay on the ground, looking up. Night was falling. He could see the dark sky and a few stars and the leaves of trees, and he felt in that instant as if reborn. A man normally given to endless bitter rumination on the past and anxiety about the future, he had no clear sense of himself as an individual as he sprawled on the cobbles. He did not feel pain. He was unperturbed by the blood that poured from his facial wounds. The flow was like a little stream of water. He lay, blissfully content.

This accident supplied him with an unexpected glimpse into what he believed to be the original state of humanity. We were all born to just such unselfconscious bliss. It was for him a most profound insight, one that confirmed and influenced all his subsequent thinking.

In other promenades, Rousseau turns to other subjects: the nature of his soul; truth and his own habit of lying about trivial things; plants and the consolation offered by the beauty of nature; his capacity for affection and friendship. The final essay, the tenth, remains unfinished, interrupted by the stroke that killed him. In this promenade he returns in imagination to Chambéry and Madame de Warens, the woman who had fostered and loved him when he was a young man making his way from Geneva and life as an unremarkable musical copyist to his mature existence as a philosopher, composer and writer in Paris.

I like these promenades. It is as though the wigs have come off, and all the posturing and point scoring has been laid aside, leaving just a man. Awkward, aware of his failings, exposed.

Of them all, it is the fifth essay that most engages me. In it, Rousseau recalls the time in 1768 when he was forced to seek refuge on a little island in the Lac de Bienne (Bielersee) in Switzerland. Some years previously he had fled from Paris to the Swiss village of Motiers to escape the condemnation of religious and civil authorities alarmed by the subversive nature of his novel *Emile* and the political implications of his Social Contract. Motiers, despite its rural setting, proved every bit as intolerant. Rousseau and his mistress, Thérèse, did little to ingratiate themselves with the conservative locals. They were clearly unmarried lovers, though they pretended to be otherwise. She was rude, and Rousseau went about clad in a lilac silk burnous with a fur-trimmed cap and entertained a succession of eccentric guests. The local pastor was the kind of firebrand still around today, given to preaching sermons to Old Testament texts that were calculated to inflame his audience. (He had already sent two men to the flames for supposedly practising witchcraft.) When the locals began throwing stones at the roof of their rented house, it was clearly time for Rousseau and Thérèse to leave.

The Île de Saint-Pierre offered consolation. It was tiny and covered in fields, woods, and vineyards where the harvest was in full swing when they arrived. The two months spent there were to prove among the most idyllic in Rousseau's life. He had had his books sent from Paris, but in the event he did not even bother to unpack them, nor set up his writing desk. Instead, he walked about the island, examining the plants. He had heard of a German scholar who had written an entire book on the subject of lemon peel (so the modern taste for books about cod or salt is not so new after all), and for a while he thought of following suit. He would divide the island into squares and examine each square minutely with the aid of a magnifying glass. He would write about the small world he found there. But instead idleness overwhelmed him. He simply walked about with no particular plan. At noon, he returned to the house to dine. In the afternoons, he rowed out onto the lake, shipped the oars and drifted. The evenings were spent sitting by the lake listening to the water lapping, and giving himself over to the delicious sensation of not thinking.

Nowhere, of course, does he mention Thérèse, the former laundry maid with whom he lived for thirty-three years and who bore him five babies, all consigned to almost certain death in the brusque care of the Parisian orphanage of Les Enfants-Trouvés. The orphanage received unwanted babies, farming them out to wet nurses in nearby villages to raise until, in theory, they were old enough to return to the city to learn a useful trade. In fact, a huge majority — well over seventy per cent — died. The fate of Thérèse's babies is unknown.

It's appalling. Even his contemporaries thought him at worst brutal and at best inconsistent: here was a man who theorised about an idealised 'natural' education for children, while behaving with a most unnatural indifference to his own. He admitted, moreover, that it had taken some effort to persuade the children's mother to follow this callous course. What this might have meant in practice, in the little household in Paris in 1746, 1747, 1748, 1751 and 1752, one can barely imagine. Her voice remains inaudible, her presence visible only in the observations of others. Yet she remained loyally at the philosopher's side throughout his life, cooking, according to all reports, the most delicious meals, attending to the comfort of a man who suffered from a chronic bladder infection, and presumably satisfying a sexuality that appears from his own account to have involved a good deal of spanking.

Characteristically, Rousseau describes a solitary existence on the island, but visitors record Thérèse's presence. It was she who deflected unwelcome guests, eager to meet the famous man, until the famous man himself had time to escape into a lower room through a trapdoor let into the floor, and take himself off to the woods. It was Thérèse who accompanied him on the idyllic day when they took a little boat and rowed with the steward's daughter to an even smaller island in the lake where they released rabbits to form the nucleus for a warren. It was Thérèse who cooked those meals recorded by approving visitors and made a comfortable home from yet another temporary apartment. She was there on the Île de Saint-Pierre, as she was throughout Rousseau's life. She outlived him, in fact, inheriting his papers and the royalties from his writings at his death in 1778, remarrying soon after — this time to a less illustrious thirty-four-year-old valet — and dying twenty-three years later in obscurity. If ever there was cause to regret the historic invisibility of women and their version of things, it is in reading the scanty biography of Thérèse Levasseur.

I know that in many ways Rousseau emerges from biography as a monster: capable of enormous cruelty, neglectful, self-absorbed, paranoid, egotistical. Yet it's impossible to dislike him. There is something in his painful self-analysis that engages sympathy. *Les rêveries du promeneur solitaire* is a short book, not more than a hundred pages. But it has a simple and unexpected sweetness. It felt oddly familiar when I first came upon it in the days after we had been jolted from bed by an earthquake and all my routines were tumbled down.

I was working on a book. A travel book. About walking. And now my inner map lay in shambles.

THE TEACUPS

When we meet we talk.
We spread jam on scones
and talk about the baby
crying at the end of the
corridor and bare feet
bleeding on glass.

The baby crying and
her brothers running
out into the dark and
the window that would
not open, framing
nothing.

The room is kind to us.
Its walls know it could
be them falling. The
cups and saucers know
they too could jump
from the table edge.
The window sees the
island in the harbour
that is made up entirely
of broken stuff, stone
clinking beneath the
feet like crockery.

We have fear folded
like a handkerchief in
a handbag. We stand
among the wise cups,
scars in our shoes,
telling the baby story.
Biff!

Bang!

All gone!

I like walking. It is simple — though my daughter who is
studying medicine tells me it is actually very complex. She lent
me an article about it. Walking involves an infinite number of
delicate adjustments of nerve and muscle, the body exerting
pressure on its environment in accordance with Newtonian
laws. When animals walk,

> *the body vaults up and over each stiff leg in an arc,*
> *analogous to an inverted pendulum. Kinetic energy*
> *in the first half of the stance phase is transformed into*
> *gravitational potential energy, which is partially*
> *recovered as the body falls forward and downward in*
> *the second half of the stance phase. Running, instead,*

is analogous to bouncing on a pogo stick. As a leg strikes the ground, kinetic and gravitational potential energy is temporarily stored as elastic strain energy in muscles, tendons, and ligaments and then is nearly all recovered during the propulsive second half of the stance phase.

The same mechanisms apply in a wide a variety of animals, including humans, kangaroos, dogs, lizards, crabs and cockroaches.

Running, we are a coiled spring. Walking, we are the pendulum of a clock, upside down. When we walk we reach that perfect comfortable state where the pendulum begins to swing, the legs producing a steady tick tock. In that state, we can walk for miles.

I love that tick tock. The Oxford specialist who told me I would be confined to bed for much of my adult life has so far been proved wrong. I have been free to walk out my own door, free to walk down city streets in Dunedin and New York and Christchurch and Paris and Toronto and London, free to walk round Mont Blanc and along the foothills of the Pyrenées. I have walked across the width of England and around the coastal tracks of Cornwall and Devon, along the narrow roads of Ireland between hedges of crimson fuchsia and delicately poised stone fences. I have walked through the bush in my own country and out into the sunlight of the tussock tops in that abrupt fashion that always feels like a kind of release.

I have been free, too, to write about it in prose and in poems, using words that also have their feet and go walking. The rhythms of words were traditionally described as footsteps in those patterns we had to memorise and identify in exams back at school. Te-DUM te-DUM: the iamb, unstressed short syllable, followed by a stressed long syllable. The heart beat we learned back in the womb as the blood pulsed around us in the dark. DUM DUM: the spondee, the word meaning 'a solemn drink offering', and there is the high priestess approaching, bearing her shallow cup. DUM-te. DUM-te: the trochee, a more frivolous matter altogether, the word meaning 'to run lightly, to trip'. Lasses trip, in old poems, and maidens and girls wearing Kate Greenaway bonnets in a pastel landscape.

I was writing a book about walking. A travel book, meandering, following the random habit of thought associated with a walk through a landscape. It would ramble. It would detour to examine curiosities. It would link walking with books read along the way or the things learned in conversation with strangers. I didn't have a shape for what I was doing. Normally I write to a more regular structure, but this time I was heading offroad, following my nose, seeing where it would take me. Then an earthquake shook me from bed and ripped up the map entirely. The quake sent a jagged tear right through my text. My mind was shaken.

For a while I felt lost. I lurched about, trying for a way through all this random thought. But then I came across a book by an eighteenth-century philosopher and he had written about walking too. So what I was doing had a precedent. Someone else had followed the same meandering route. I could just make out his footsteps across the hillside.

I wrote a book about walking, a book with a tear through it. A broken book.

And here we are, almost at its end. There is a light in the valley, the sound of traffic as we come down from the hill. There is a meal cooking somewhere, a soak in a warm bath or shower. We'll have a drink, happy and companionable with friends, watch the sun go down over the hills, blazing.

Last year, before the quake, I took a night class in hieroglyphics. At last I was going to find out what those little figures on the ebony box on the mantelpiece meant: the images my father had told me were actually words. Mysterious words in an old language on the box from that distant place called The War, that held precious things like the mortgage papers. The same box that now sits on the mantelpiece in my home at Otanerito. Last year I discovered at last that the little legs on that box, striding forward without the encumbrance of a torso, were actually the sign for an active verb. The glyph transforms the succeeding array of signs into action, rather than object. So, a little heart alone — just its profile with the two knobs on top that are the aortic veins — signifies just that: a heart. But alongside a pair of walking legs it means 'impatient' or 'quick of heart'.

Those legs appear at the commencement of a phrase that marks the end of any text, whether poem or something lengthier like the massive compilation titled in English *The Book of the Dead*. A truer translation of the original would be *The Book of Walking Forth*, being a book of instructions on how a human being might continue on their way, walking out from the tomb into the unseen future beyond death.

The concluding phrase to that book of instructions is the same as the concluding phrase to the eulogy painted on a tomb wall, or the poem on papyrus that celebrates the beauties of nature, or the panegyric carved into the stone face of a temple. You see the phrase everywhere. The line of images begins with a pair of legs to signify action. Then there is a quail chick in profile, that little bird I see in the mornings when I walk on the reserve, whirring away on tiny frantic feet into the dry grass beside the creek. As a hieroglyph its image is used in lieu of our dot, our full stop, to mark the end of a phrase of meaning. But here in this particular phrase of conclusion it takes on one of its other roles, as the sign for a sound somewhere between 'w' and 'u'. Following the quail chick is a horned snake above a square and a tiny unfurling frond exactly like a koru, then half a lion: just the forequarters, head and paws in profile, which signifies 'before' or 'in front of'. (The hindquarters with rump, tail and folded rear legs naturally means 'behind' or 'after'.) Beneath the forequarters of the lion is a shape like the half-profile of a round bun, or a breast, or a swollen belly, which is used to signify the feminine. The sign for 'son', for example, is a goose: the sign for a daughter is a goose accompanied by a little half-bun. Then comes another snake, the hindquarters of a lion and a final snake. The entire phrase is translated by modern scholars as 'iu-ef pu hat-ef pehwy-fy' and it means: 'The text has come from its beginning to its end.'

And so it has.

THE LIMIT

There is no limit.
No cut-off point.
No closing chord.
No red line marked
to say The End.

The seas can gather
themselves up into
columns of blue
light hung with
pretty fish.

And someone can
suffer, her beauty
peeled to the pith.
And someone can
wash ashore wearing
only one shoe, wet
lick of hair at bare
neck.

And the sea can still
fall and the hills can
shout and tear them

selves asunder and
whole bands of
children disappear
and towns and plans
and yes, you too,
all you
pretty fish.

And then there's love.
No limit.

Works consulted and quoted from in this book include:

Travels with a Donkey in the Cévennes by Robert Louis Stevenson.
  Penguin Books, 2004
Robert Louis Stevenson by Claire Harman. HarperCollins, 2004
Mentone and the Riviera as a Winter Climate by James Henry Bennet.
  John Churchill, 1861
Winter in the South of Europe by James Henry Bennet. John Churchill,
  1865
Winter in Majorca by George Sand. Cassell, 1956
The White Death: A History of Tuberculosis by Thomas Dormandy.
  Hambledon & London, 2002
*The Forgotten Plague: How the Battle against Tuberculosis was
  Won — and Lost* by Frank Ryan. Little, Brown, 1992
The Garden Party, and Other Stories by Katherine Mansfield.
  Alfred A. Knopf, 1922
Candide by Voltaire. Penguin Books, 1947
'The Earthquake at Lisbon' by Charles Davy. Available at:
  www.fordham.edu/halsall/mod/1755lisbonquake.asp
Reveries of the Solitary Walker by Jean-Jacques Rousseau. Penguin
  Books, 1979
*Jean-Jacques Rousseau: The Early Life and Work of Jean-Jacques
  Rousseau 1712–1754* by Maurice Cranston. Allen Lane, 1983
Jean-Jacques Rousseau: Restless Genius by Leo Damrosch, Houghton
  Mifflin, 2005
'Motor Patterns in Human Walking and Running' by G. Cappellini,
  Y. P. Ivanenko, R. E. Poppele and F. Lacquaniti. American
  Physiological Society, *Journal of Neurophysiology*, June 2006,
  vol. 95, no. 6